Imperialism, Racism, and Development Theories

Hilmar Kaiser

•

Imperialism, Racism, and Development Theories

The Construction of a Dominant Paradigm on Ottoman Armenians

Gomidas Institute
Ann Arbor, Michigan

An earlier version of the text of this book was presented at "The Sassoun Massacre: A Hundred Year Perspective," a Marie Manoogian History Seminar held in Ann Arbor, Michigan, on 10 September 1994, organized by Professor Ronald Grigor Suny, Ara Sarafian, and Vincent Lima, and cosponsored by the University of Michigan Armenian Studies Program and the *Armenian Review.*

Gomidas Institute, PO Box 4218, Ann Arbor, Michigan 48106-4218, USA
© 1997 by the Gomidas Institute
All Rights Reserved. Published 1998

Printed in the United States of America

04 03 02 01 00 99   5 4 3 2

ISBN 1-884630-02-2

Please address questions and comments to the following address:

Gomidas Institute
PO Box 208
Princeton NJ 08542-0208
USA

Phone: 1-609-883-9222
Fax: 1-609-883-9277
Email: books@gomidas.org

CONTENTS

FOREWORD

Hilmar Kaiser's important essay could not be more timely, for it deconstructs some of the central statements of modern Ottoman historiography. These include the views that the economic success of the Ottoman Armenian bourgeoisie stemmed from their unscrupulous character and European privileges, that this success prevented the economic development of the empire, and that it provoked the Turks into getting rid of the Armenian people.

Kaiser's approach reminds one of Nietzsche's *On the Genealogy of Morals* in that he traces ideas back to their origins to unveil their ideological content and the interests they conceal. These origins he finds in the racist and nationalist propaganda which developed in German imperialist circles as early as the 1890s. In particular, Kaiser emphasizes the central role played in modern historiography by the writings of one such German propagandist, Alphons Sussnitzki. Translated into English in the 1960s by Charles Issawi, a prominent economic historian of the Middle East, Sussnitzki's essays have since then been often quoted by Middle East scholars either ignorant or dismissive of the context in which they were produced. Sussnitzki has thus been fetishized, treated as if his works were based on solid, irrefutable research.

Kaiser shows that Turkish and Western scholars from diverse ideological horizons adopted these ideas to various degrees and adapted them to their theories. Among them, one finds Turkish

nationalists of the so-called Kadro school in the 1930s, proponents of the liberal modernization theory in the 1950s and
1960s, and both Turkish and Western followers of Immanuel
Wallerstein's assertedly Marxist world-system theory from the
1970s on. Kaiser's argument is especially strong where it exam-
ines the Kadro movement and world-system theory, for scholars
from both of these schools readily subscribe to the stereotypes
about non-Muslim Ottomans in general and Armenians in particular. Although modernization theory, as represented by
Issawi's writings, also echoes the views expressed by German
imperialists and Turkish nationalists, it does so merely to explain
the perceptions and frame of mind of the Ottoman elite.

The analysis of the strange convergence of opinions about
Armenians among racist German imperialists, Turkish nationalists, and Marxist followers of world-system theory is clearly Kaiser's central contribution. It reveals that world-system theory, so
dominant in contemporary Ottoman historiography, is but a
perverted form of Marxism catering to the interests of Turkish
nationalists and of the Turkish state. As such, world-system theory converges, on the left side of the political spectrum, with the
views of right-wing Turkish and Western historians who deny
the Armenian Genocide or explain it away in euphemistic terms
as the result of Armenian political provocations. In the world-
system perspective, indeed, the economic achievements of the
Ottoman Armenian bourgeoisie are one more provocation on the
part of devious and exploitative minorities who did not shun col-
laborating with Western capitalism. Clearly, the exploited Turks
had to do something to free themselves and their state from such
a nuisance.

It is striking that these assertedly Marxist historians and sociol-
ogists never mention that peasants formed 70 to 75 percent of all
Ottoman Armenians and that craftspeople and downtrodden
migrant workers made up the overwhelming majority of the

urban Armenian population. Kurds, for their part, are simply left out of Ottoman historiography altogether, although they constituted a plurality in the eastern provinces.[1]

As the intellectual and ideological links among various ideas can often be traced back almost *ad infinitum,* the genealogy of ideas is a difficult endeavor. In this case, one could explore the possibility that German racist perceptions of the Armenians were themselves rooted in and infected by Ottoman prejudice toward that people, manifested for instance in many stereotypical idioms and sayings about Armenians.[2] These stereotypes, which pre-existed the period of Turkish nationalism starting at the turn of the century, were subsequently coated in a more theoretical language and integrated into the economic program of the Young Turks. *Millî Iktisat* (National Economy), as it was called, was inspired by the ideas of the German nationalist Friedrich List (1789–1846). The goal of National Economy in its Ottoman context was to rid the economy of its "parasitic" non-Turkish elements and to create an "organic" Turkish bourgeoisie that would lead the empire to economic success. In addition to Turkism and Pan-Turkism, *Millî Iktisat* was the third ideological motivation and justification for the Armenian Genocide. It would be interesting to know whether German propaganda and cooperation with the Young Turks shaped the elaboration of this theory and,

1. For an extended treatment of the uses and abuses of world-system theory in the historiography of the Ottoman Empire, see Stephan Astourian, *Testing World-System Theory, Cilicia (1830s–1890s): Armenian-Turkish Polarization and the Ideology of Modern Ottoman Historiography,* Ph.D. diss., UCLA, 1996 (Ann Arbor, Mich: UMI Publications, 1997).

2. See, among others, Alfred Körte, *Anatolische Skizzen* (Berlin: Julius Springer, 1896), pp. 53–59, 62; and Ernst Jäckh, *Der aufsteigende Halbmond: Beitrage sur türkischen Renaissance* (Berlin: Buchverlag der 'Hilfe,' 1911), pp. 99–101.

more importantly perhaps, its application during the First World War.[3]

Since the current historiography of the empire is based on older stereotypes, albeit garbed in social-scientific language, Kaiser concludes that "social history has been unable to criticize and revise Turkish nationalist views" and that "a critical social history of the Ottoman social formation is still a desideratum" (pp. 58–59). He is right.

STEPHAN H. ASTOURIAN
University of California, Los Angeles

3. On Friedrich List, see Roman Szporluk, *Communism & Nationalism: Karl Marx versus Friedrich List* (Oxford and New York: Oxford University Press, 1988). On Millî Iktisat, see Zafer Toprak, *Türkiye'de "Milli Iktisat" (1908–1918)* (Ankara: Yurt Yayıncılık, 1982).

1
INTRODUCTION

Although the social history of Armenians in the Ottoman Empire has yet to be written, Armenians are discussed in numerous recent publications on Ottoman social and economic history. Indeed, the role Ottoman Armenians played in trade is at the center of a lively debate about the integration of the Ottoman Empire into the world economy. A striking feature of this debate is the degree to which works by authors of different and sometimes opposing theoretical schools agree in their negative assessment of that role. Close scrutiny of these works reveals that many prominent authors have been influenced by the work of Alphons Sussnitzki, a German writer who published an article in 1917 on a supposed Ottoman "division of labor according to nationality." Without questioning Sussnitzki's own ideological position or the political context in which he wrote, these authors have used Sussnitzki's work as an important source for their accounts of late Ottoman social history.

Drawing on his own research on the Ottoman working class, Donald Quataert has already demonstrated the untenability of Sussnitzki's statements.[1] The present study will discuss the his-

1. "There is truth to the assertion that ethnic groups dominated crafts. In Ottoman Salonica, for example, Jews formed the vast majority of the porters and of the labor force in general, and Turkish Muslims prevailed in Usak generally and in its rug industry in particular. If Turkish Muslims were the majority of the rugmakers

torical background to Sussnitzki's racist work and the reproduction of Sussnitzki's assertions in more recent histories of the Ottoman Empire. It will demonstrate that Sussnitzki's work was part of a tradition of German anti-Armenian propaganda that emerged in response to German foreign-policy needs after the 1880s. The study will trace the impact of Sussnitzki's article on Ottoman historiography.

GERMAN INTERESTS IN THE OTTOMAN EMPIRE, 1871–96

The Ottoman Empire did not begin to play a central role in the political strategies of the German government until almost two decades after the formation, in 1871, of the German Kaiserreich. Chancellor Bismarck's statement that German interests in the Ottoman Empire were not worth the bones of a single Pomeranian grenadier sums up the official German attitude toward the Ottoman state.[2] In Bismarck's political worldview, the Ottoman Empire was but a means of diverting the imperialist interests of the other Great Powers—Russia, Great Britain, and France. Bismarck hoped that the attention of these powers, with their designs for the Middle East, would be distracted from Germany,

---

in Usak, Christians made most of the rugs in Konya. Making statements about such Jewish or Muslim or Christian control in such specific places is one thing; but it is quite another to incorrectly surmise from such facts the presence of a general ethnic division of labor. There simply was not a widespread ethnic division of labor: Particular groups generally did not control or dominate particular activities in the Ottoman Empire as a whole. The nineteenth century Ottoman labor force was neither largely Turkish, Armenian, nor Greek, and it was not primarily Muslim, Christian, or Jewish. An ethnic or religious group that dominated an economic activity in one particular region did not necessarily do so in another." Donald Quataert, "The Social History Of Labor in the Ottoman Empire: 1800–1914," in *The Social History of Labor in the Middle East,* ed. Ellis Jay Goldberg (Boulder, Colo.: Westview, 1996), pp. 31–32.

2. Gregor Schöllgen, *Imperialismus und Gleichgewicht. Deutschland, England und die orientalische Frage 1871–1914* (Munich: Oldenbourg, 1984), p. 16.

and resulting rivalries would benefit the German position in Central Europe. German involvement in Ottoman affairs was to be avoided or, at least, limited.[3] During the late 1880s, however, the situation changed. With the deterioration of Russian-German relations, German diplomats felt free to engage themselves more actively in Ottoman affairs. Soon German businesspeople realized the economic potential of the Ottoman market. A German group led by the Deutsche Bank secured a concession for the construction of a railway line in the Ottoman Empire. The new line was to link Constantinople with Angora. As concessions for the construction of another railway line toward Baghdad seemed to be within reach, German attitudes toward the Ottoman Empire underwent profound change.

The progress of the railway project was followed closely by German public opinion. It led to a wave of publications on the economic potential of the Ottoman Empire. The enthusiasm, however, was not as spontaneous as it first appeared. The Anatolian Railway Company discreetly supported the visits of German scholars and other writers to its line in order to secure public attention in Germany for its operations. The Deutsche Bank, owner of the railway company, must have hoped for economic and political benefits from this exercise.[4] Once awakened, how-

3. For an overview, see Matthew Smith Anderson, *The Eastern Question, 1774–1923: A Study in International Relations* (London: Macmillan, 1966; 2d rev. ed., 1968).

4. Roman Oberhummer and Heinrich Zimmerer, eds., *Durch Syrien und Kleinasien. Reiseschilderungen und Studien* (Berlin: Reimer, 1899), pp. 23–24; Hans-Hermann von Schweinitz, *In Kleinasien. Ein Reitausflug durch das Innere Kleinasiens im Jahre 1905* (Berlin: Reimer, 1906), pp. 57–58 On the economic difficulties of the Deutsche Bank in 1893, see Arthur von Gwinner, *Lebenserinnerungen*, ed. Manfred Pohl (Frankfurt am Main: Knapp, 1975), p. 61. On German Middle East propaganda, see Wilhelm van Kampen, "Studien zur deutschen Türkeipolitik in der Zeit Wilhelms II." (Ph.D. diss., Christian-Albrechts-Universität Kiel, 1968); Gregor Schöllgen, "'Dann müssen wir uns aber Mesopotamien sicher!' Motive deutscher

ever, German public interest got out of control and, much to the distress of the bank directors, a lively debate developed on the prospects for German settlements along the Anatolian Railway.[5]

The views of the German Foreign Office (Auswärtiges Amt) were more realistic than the visions of German "Orient" propagandists. Nevertheless, the economic importance of the Ottoman Empire as a market for German exports and investments was now well understood. In order to protect the gains anticipated from existing concessions and to strengthen the German position within the Ottoman economy in general, the German government sought to protect the territorial integrity of the Ottoman state. Clearly, this effort did not stem from any genuine sympathy for the Ottoman sultan and the political establishment in Constantinople, but from a fear that Germany had more to lose than to win from a dismembering of the empire. Thus, the Ottoman government could count on a certain measure of German support in case of diplomatic conflicts with other European pow-

---

Türkeipolitik zur Zeit Wilhelm II. in zeitgenössischen Darstellungen," *Saeculum* 32 (1981), pp. 130–45; Fikret Adanır, "Wandlungen des deutschen Türkeibildes in der ersten Hälfte des 20. Jahrhunderts," *Zeitschrift für Türkeistudien* 4 (1991), pp. 195–211. An alternative interpretation has been advanced by Lothar Rathmann; see, for instance, Rathmann, "Zur Legende vom 'antikolonialen' Charakter der Bagdadbahnpolitik in der wilhelminischen Ära des deutschen Monopolkapitalismus," *Zeitschrift für Geschichtswissenschaft* 9 (1961), pp. 246–71.

5. See, for instance, Karl Kärger, *Kleinasien, Ein deutsches Kolonisationsfeld. Kolonialwirthschaftliche Studie* (Berlin: Gergonne & Cie., 1892); Reinhold Menz, *Deutsche Arbeit in Kleinasien. Reiseskizze und Wirthschaftsstudie* (Berlin: Springer, 1893); Ernst Oehlmann, *Ist es möglich die deutsche Auswanderung nach Kleinasien zu lenken?* Sammlung gemeinverständlicher wissenschaftlicher Vorträge, Neue Folge, 8. Serie, Heft 188 (Hamburg: Verlagsanstalt und Druckerei A.G., 1894); Max Schlagintweit, *Deutsche Kolonisationsbestrebungen in Kleinasien. Vortrag gehalten in der Deutschen Kolonial-Gesellschaft, Abteilung Berlin, am 9. Januar 1900* (Munich: Wolf & Sohn, 1900). The bank's resistance against any German colonization scheme was publicly criticized by the German extreme political right; see Albrecht Wirth, *Türkei und Persien,* Streiflichter auf die Weltpolitik von Albrecht Wirth, Heft 2 (Frankfurt am Main–Berlin: Diesterweg, 1908), p. 14.

ers. From 1894 onward, the steady convergence in the interests of the Ottoman and German governments also became a crucial factor in the development of the Armenian Question.[6]

In 1878, the Armenian Question was an important issue at the Congress of Berlin, although promised reforms in the "Armenian provinces" of the Ottoman Empire did not materialize at that time. In the early 1890s, however, the formation of the Hamidieh, Kurdish cavalry units named after the sultan, and the appearance of Armenian revolutionary organizations marked a turn in the course of events. In the eastern provinces, the living conditions of the Armenian peasantry became increasingly precarious, as numerous Kurdish tribes—many of them officially courted by the government—came to arrangements with corrupt local Ottoman administrators in pursuit of their sectarian interests vis-à-vis Armenians. Consequently, Armenian revolutionaries sought to organize popular resistance among Armenian peasants against the oppressive rule of certain Kurdish tribes.[7]

Thus, when in 1893 Armenian villagers in the Sasun area, objecting to double taxation, refused to pay the taxes levied by both the Ottoman state and Kurdish chieftains, what might have been simply a local conflict took on a wider significance. Crucial in this regard was the fact that the Armenians of Sasun managed to repel the attacks of the Kurdish tribes and thus brought the established exploitative system into question. The presence of a number of Armenian revolutionaries in Sasun further increased the importance of these events.

6. Norbert Saupp, "Das Deutsche Reich und die Armenische Frage 1878–1914" (Ph.D. diss., Köln, 1990), p. 47.

7. Henry Finnis Blosse Lynch, *Armenia. Travels and Studies,* vol. 2 (London, 1901; reprint, Beirut: Khayats, 1965), p. 5.

In the spring and summer of 1894, the Ottoman state intensified its military presence in the Sasun region.[8] In June 1894, the Ottoman authorities tried in vain to arrest the Armenian leaders of the region and thus decapitate the organized resistance. As a result, the situation took a turn for the worse as Armenians and Kurds clashed in the mountains of Sasun. By August the stage was set for a major encounter between the Armenian defenders of Sasun on the one hand and the attacking Kurdish tribes and Ottoman troops on the other. Given the military superiority of the attackers, the outcome of the confrontation was predictable. Realizing that the Ottoman state was trying to eradicate their community, the Armenians fought a determined last-trench defense but could not prevent a massacre of the surviving men, women, and children who were unable to escape to hiding places in the surrounding mountains. Estimates of the number of victims vary between nine hundred and three thousand.[9]

The Sasun massacre was the first organized mass slaughter of an Ottoman Armenian community in the 1890s. During the next two years, numerous urban and rural Armenian communities became victims of other organized massacres. When in August 1896 a group of Armenian revolutionaries occupied the Ottoman Bank in Constantinople, the government had simply prepared a bloodbath in the capital in anticipation of the event.

8. See the reports reproduced in Ertuğrul Zekâi Ökte, *Ottoman Archives: Yildiz Collection: The Armenian Question*, vol. 1, *Talori Incidents* (Istanbul: T. T. T. The Historical Research Foundation, 1989).

9. For an account of the events based primarily on British sources, see Christopher Walker, *Armenia: The Survival of a Nation*, rev. 2d ed. (New York: St. Martin's Press, 1990), pp. 136–48. Rouben Ter-Minassian recorded the events as described to him by survivors about ten years later; Ter-Minassian, *Mémoires d'un cadre révolutionnaire arménien*, trans. Souren L. Chanth (Athens: F. R. A. Dachnaktsoutioun, 1994), pp. 243–52. Many survivors were forcibly deported from the area and died on the march to Urfa. In Urfa the Armenian community organized a relief campaign; see the memoirs of an Armenian physician, Avedis Nakashian, *A Man Who Found a Country* (New York: Crowell, 1940), pp. 135–36.

These atrocities provoked international reaction, European public opinion was deeply disturbed, and the signatory powers to the Treaty of Berlin considered taking diplomatic action.[10]

During this crisis the German government remained faithful to its strategy of opposing international intervention in the Ottoman Empire. Although Wilhelm II, the German emperor, more than once denounced the massacres, the German government tacitly supported the sultan and obstructed the combined actions of the Powers.[11]

10. In his memoirs, the editor of *Konstantinopler Handelsblatt* gave a detailed description of the Constantinople massacre. He stressed how the slaughter had been organized by the Ottoman authorities. Hugo von Köller, *Von Pasewalk zum Bosporus. Ein abenteuerliches Junkerleben* (Berlin-Leipzig: Brunnen Verlag, 1927), pp. 245–48.

11. Schöllgen, *Imperialismus und Gleichgewicht*, pp. 69–71.

2

THE DEVELOPMENT OF GERMAN RACIAL STEREOTYPES OF ARMENIANS

During the Armenian massacres of 1894–96, the German government did not limit itself to impeding international sanctions against the Ottoman Empire and to obstructing British attempts to introduce reforms. It went beyond these defensive maneuvers and embarked on a policy of denouncing the critics of the Ottoman government. Wilhelm II set the tone personally. On 20 December 1895, Wilhelm II met with the British military attaché Colonel Swaine. Wilhelm alleged that the Armenian reform scheme was intended to destabilize the rule of the sultan. Estimating that eighty thousand Armenians had been massacred to date, the emperor wondered whether any Armenians remained, and he asked Swaine whether England was not yet worried by the consequences its policy wrought upon the Armenian population. In short, Wilhelm simply accused the British of being responsible for the Armenian massacres.[12]

12. Wolfgang J. Mommsen, *Grossmachtstellung und Weltpolitik 1870–1914. Die Außenpolitik des Deutschen Reiches* (Frankfurt am Main–Berlin: Ullstein, 1993), p. 129; for the same accusation see the comments of Wilhelm II in a letter from Ambassador Saurma to Chancellor Hohenlohe, Pera, 12 Dec. 1895, no. 227, in *Die Große Politik der europäischen Kabinette,* ed. Johannes Lepsius, Albrecht Mendelssohn-Bartholdy, and Friedrich Thimme, vol. 9 (Berlin: Deutsche Verlagsanstalt für Politik und Geschichte, 1927) pp. 119–20, document no. 2471.

The British government was not the only one to blame in the official German view. In a draft memorandum, the German Foreign Office official Alfons Mumm sketched the German position on the Armenian Question in the following terms:

> Despite all [our] sympathy for the present sad condition of the Armenians, one must not forget that the characteristics of this race, its cunningness, and its rebellious activities had to provoke the rage of the Turks, and much has happened that could allow the Turks to assume that they were [acting] in self-defense.[13]

In attributing the causes of the Armenian massacres to the "racial characteristics" of the victims, Mumm exonerated the Ottoman government from blame and the German government from responsibility. Mumm's explanation of the Armenian massacres was, however, not of his own creation. In fact, he had taken up an ethnic stereotype that already existed in German public opinion. Such stereotypes of Armenians were products of contemporary discussions of German colonization of the Ottoman Empire.

Alfred Körte

Shortly before Mumm wrote his memorandum, the German archaeologist Alfred Körte published a series of articles on the Ottoman Empire in a conservative German newspaper. He reported his impressions, gained during a visit to the Anatolian railway in 1894–95, and his description of Armenians had strong repercussions in German public opinion.[14] Stating that he did

---

13. Draft by Mumm in *Auswärtiges Amt—Politisches Archiv Orientalia Generalia no. 5,* vol. 30, 26 Nov. 1896, as quoted in Saupp, "Das Deutsche Reich und die Armenische Frage," p. 111.

14. The articles were then published as a book: Alfred Körte, *Anatolische Skizzen* (Berlin: Springer, 1896). On the repercussions, see Saupp, "Das Deutsche Reich und die Armenische Frage," p.141; Oberhummer and Zimmerer, *Durch Syrien und Kleinasien,* pp. 21–22, qualify Körte's statements, which had caused some uproar,

not want to excuse the Armenian massacres, he maintained nevertheless that Armenians had long provoked Turkish resentment and had thus brought about their own sad fate. Armenian merchants, for example, were accused of exploiting and abusing the Turkish peasantry. This, according to Körte, was not only an economic matter but one of racial character as well. Körte believed that Armenians lied and stole without the slightest scruple and that it was "possible to state that where one is cheated in Anatolia, one is dealing with Armenians."[15] In fact, according to Körte, Armenians would perform all kinds of cheating as sport. The archaeologist stressed the moral corruptness of Armenians in even stronger terms. He claimed that, according to his information, Armenian men in the provinces of Van and Bitlis would leave their young wives behind and would not mind if the household grew during their absence. Körte's strong words were intended to be a warning to German businesspeople, too: Given the bad characteristics of Armenians, and to a lesser extent those of Greeks, cooperation with these people would necessarily lead to the swindling of German businesspeople. Therefore, Germans should try to win the confidence of Turks and other Muslims and secure sound bases for their business enterprises. In sum, Körte suggested that both Turks and Germans had reason to oppose Armenians. He tried to undermine German Christian solidarity with Armenians by showing that Armenians were not good Christians. For readers with more practical interests, Körte offered the implicit conclusion that the weakening of the Armenian position in the Ottoman Empire would create benefits for German economic interests.[16]

---

as "hard," but nevertheless consider the archaeologist an insightful judge of human nature.

15. Körte, *Anatolische Skizzen*, p. 52: "Man kann schlechthinsagen, wo man in Anatolien betrogen wird, hat man es mit Armeniern zu thun."

16. Körte, *Anatolische Skizzen*, pp. 53, 57–58, 59, 89–90. The idea that Armenians and Greeks were an important obstacle to German economic penetration was

"Morality" and "German interests" remained the focus of German public debate on the Armenian Question. The German government tried to silence undesirable statements and Protestant grassroots support for Ottoman Armenians. By 1898, however, some Protestant German politicians had overcome the contradiction between Christian solidarity with Armenians and German political interests. The year before, the German government had announced its intention of following a new policy of *Weltpolitik* (world politics).[17] This catchword referred to the German claim to a part in all international decisions concerning the colonial partition of the world. The first popular and spectacular manifestation of this policy was the "pilgrimage" of Wilhelm II to Palestine and his visit to Constantinople.[18] The emperor, a rather unbalanced man, was impressed by his reception in the Ottoman capital.[19] In Damascus he declared that Germany was the protector of the world's Muslim population. This statement was bound to have a negative impact on German diplomatic relations with those of the Great Powers that ruled over substantial Muslim populations: Britain, France, and Russia. In Germany, the emperor's declaration served as a signal to the Pan-German

---

not new. Kärger had already stressed such concerns, adding that Armenians supported Germany's enemy, France. Kärger, *Kleinasien, Ein deutsches Kolonisationsfeld*, pp. 68, 70.

17. Michael Fröhlich, *Imperialismus. Deutsche Kolonial- und Weltpolitik 1880–1914, Deutsche Geschichte der neuesten Zeit vom 19. Jahrhundert bis zur Gegenwart* (Munich: Deutsch-Türkische Vereinigung, 1994), pp. 73–89.

18. For a discussion of the visit, see Nazaret Naltchayan, "Kaiser Wilhelm II's Visits to the Ottoman Empire: Rationale, Reactions and the Meaning of Images," *Armenian Review* 42, no. 166 (1989), pp. 47–78.

19. On Wilhelm II's personality, see John C. G. Röhl, "The Emperor's New Clothes: A Character Sketch of Kaiser Wilhelm II," in *Kaiser Wilhelm II: New Interpretations*, ed. John C. G. Röhl and Nicolaus Sombart (Cambridge: Cambridge Univ. Press, 1982), pp. 23–61.

League to give up its hopes and agitation for German colonies in the Ottoman Middle East.[20]

FRIEDRICH NAUMANN

Kaiser Wilhelm's visit was an outstanding event for the German press. Numerous German journalists accompanied the imperial family and reported on their travels at length. One of these journalists was the German national-liberal politician Friedrich Naumann. Soon, as in Körte's case, his articles appeared in slightly expanded form as a book. This book, entitled *Asia,* became a bestseller and was one of the most widely read volumes of its time. It gave much space to the German role in the Ottoman Empire and also touched upon the Armenian Question. For Naumann, too, the fate of the Armenian population was part of the larger question of the future of the Ottoman Empire. The author presented the Armenian massacres as an act of understandable imperial self-defense: The purpose of the massacres had been to weaken the Armenian population numerically so that they would not be able to act politically for some time. Naumann stressed that supporting Armenians was tantamount to supporting Britain, and this was damaging to German interests since Germany was still too weak to occupy Ottoman territory. Instead, Naumann pointed out, Germany had more to gain from economic cooperation with the Ottoman Empire, as the economies of the two states would complement each other.[21]

---

20. Horst Gründer, "Die Kaiserfahrt Wilhelms II. ins Heilige Land 1898. Aspekte deutscher Palästinapolitik im Zeitalter des Imperialismus," in *Weltpolitik, Europagedanke, Regionalismus. Festschrift Heinz Gollwitzer zum 65. Geburtstag am 30. Januar 1982,* ed. Heinz Dollinger, Horst Gründer, and Alwin Hanschmidt (Münster: Aschendorff, 1982), p. 380; Fröhlich, *Imperialismus,* p. 87. Expecting the partition of the Ottoman Empire, the Pan-German League had published its colonial demands in 1896; see All-Deutscher Verband, ed., *Deutschlands Ansprüche an das Türkische Erbe* (Munich: Lehmann, 1896).

21. Friedrich Naumann, *"Asia." Eine Orientreise über Athen, Konstantinopel, Baalbek, Nazareth, Jerusalem, Kairo, Neapel,* 7th ed. (Berlin: Hilfe, 1913), pp. 137–

Naumann did not limit himself to economic and geopolitical considerations. Like Körte, he tried to support his analysis with comments on alleged Armenian racial characteristics. Putting his remarks in the mouth of an anonymous German potter living in Constantinople, Naumann radicalized Körte's statements. He maintained that Armenian men did not just leave their families behind but actually sold their wives and young daughters. He claimed that Armenians also stole from their own brothers. In short, he reported, Armenians were morally contaminating Constantinople. Naumann let his potter add that Armenians in rural areas were no better. Commenting on German Protestant associations that educated Armenian orphans who had survived the recent massacres, he stated that German philanthropy was wasted on these orphans since they too would become like the others. For him, only Catholic Armenians had redeeming qualities.[22]

The opinions Naumann expressed closely corresponded with German official views, which were critical of German material support for Ottoman Armenians. Catholic Armenians were excluded from criticism in the interests of mollifying German Catholic circles; and the thesis of the Ottoman government's self-defense was seemingly confirmed by Naumann's alleged German observer. The publication of Naumann's book demonstrated that Protestant national-liberal circles supported the foreign policy of the government and, moreover, shared the racist views of government officials and conservatives like Körte. In

40, 160–63. The author developed the image of the Ottoman Empire as a supplier of raw materials and a market for German finished products.

22. Naumann felt obliged to add that he did not share the views of the potter; pp. 31–32, 135. For public reaction to the book, see Kampen, "Studien zur deutschen Türkeipolitik," p. 122. Paul Rohrbach, who was to become one of the major German liberal imperialists before World War I, took up Naumann's theses. He argued, however, that German relief efforts on behalf of Armenians were in harmony with the objects of German Middle East policies and would facilitate German economic penetration. Rohrbach, "Deutschland unter den Armeniern," *Preussische Jahrbücher* 96 (1899), pp. 308–9, 318, 321, 328.

1899, the anti-Armenian attitudes of the German government were confirmed when the emperor's chamberlain published an account of Wilhelm II's visit to Palestine, inserting pejorative remarks about Armenians and Greeks.[23]

By the turn of the twentieth century the German public had become used to racist statements about Armenians by scholars, politicians, and representatives of the imperial court. These statements were used as a tool to exonerate the Ottoman government from any guilt and to serve German economic and political interests in the Ottoman Empire.

HUGO GROTHE

In 1903 the Ottoman government granted the long-awaited concession for the Baghdad Railway to a German group, and hopes for a bright German future in the Middle East gained new impetus. In the following years the Armenian Question did not seem to threaten German interests and disappeared from the debates of German "Orient" propagandists. However, ethnic stereotyping continued and began appearing in German academic writing. In 1902, Hugo Grothe, one of the most noted German "Orient" propagandists, published his doctoral thesis in which he argued that from the perspective of German colonization, the Baghdad Railway in Northern Syria formed an essential, "national field of activity."[24] The author expressed his "national hopes" that it would be possible to establish autonomous German settlements in the Ottoman Empire which would not

23. Mirbach maintained that Armenians had provoked disturbances in order to embarrass the Ottoman government. Moreover, he claimed, they were exploiters too. Ernst Frhr. von Mirbach, *Reise des Kaisers und der Kaiserin nach Palästina. Drei Vorträge* (Berlin: Mittler & Sohn, 1899), p. 107.

24. Hugo Grothe, "Die Bagdadbahn und das schwäbische Bauernelement in Transkaukasien und Palästina" (Inaugural-Dissertation, Würzburg, 1902; Munich: Lehmann, 1902), pp. 4, 10–11, 16-17, 55. Grothe understood his study as a further development of the views the propagandists of the 1890s; see pp. 15–16.

resemble an outright German acquisition of Ottoman territory. Referring to the problems of already existing German colonies in Transcaucasia, Grothe stressed the importance of purely German settlements and the need to keep "alien races" out of them. In this context, he singled out Armenians as important enemies in German colonization efforts. Armenians were said to have destroyed or damaged German settlements by cheating and usury.[25]

Discussing Ottoman Armenians, Grothe stated that it was their bloodsucking activities and not Muslim "religious fanaticism" that were the real causes for the Armenian massacres of the 1890s.[26] However, Grothe made it clear that only Armenians in Ottoman port cities should be blamed—and not those living on their soil in the Armenian provinces of the empire. Here Grothe put the responsibility for the massacres on those Armenian "racial brothers" who did not live in the very rural poverty that Grothe denounced.[27] In a later pamphlet Grothe went so far as to say that the perpetrators of massacres were only taking back, admittedly in a violent manner, that which had been taken from them illegally by their Armenian subordinates.[28]

PAUL GEISTER

"Armenian usury" was also a central theme in the work of Paul Geister. In his thesis on the integration of the Ottoman Empire into international markets, Geister discussed German economic expansion into the region. He elaborated on the accusation that

25. Ibid., pp. 24, 28.
26. Hugo Grothe, *Auf türkischer Erde. Reisebilder und Studien* (Berlin: Allgemeiner Verein für Deutsche Litteratur, 1903), p. 275.
27. Ibid., pp. 49–50.
28. Hugo Grothe, *Die asiatische Türkei und die deutschen Interessen. Gedanken zur inneren Umgestaltung des osmanischen Reiches und zu den Zielen der deutschen Kulturpolitik,* Der Neue Orient, Heft 9 (Halle: Gebauer-Schwedtsche Druckerei, 1913), p. 16.

Armenians were usurers and linked them to British economic interests, thus developing the image of an Armenian alliance with one of Germany's chief competitors in international markets. At this point, ethnic stereotyping integrated elements of economics, political science, and racism, and thereby covered important fields of German public discourse of the time.[29]

ALBRECHT WIRTH

The close connection between scholarship, journalism, and propaganda was also exemplified in the writings of Albrecht Wirth, a university professor in Munich and a leading member of the anti-Semitic Pan-German League. Having published travelogues in various German newspapers, Wirth had gained a wide audience for his views on international relations. His articles were often published in book form, too, and some texts were republished with only minor changes.[30] Wirth's assessment of Russian and Ottoman Armenians was a collection of accusations: Armenians were enjoying British government support for smuggling arms while the American college in Constantinople was a hotbed for anarchism. Wirth denied that Armenians had been suppressed, and stated that they were the real culprits, having pro-

29. Paul Geister, "Die Türkei im Rahmen der Weltwirtschaft" (Ph.D. diss., Greifswald, 1907), p. 45.

30. Compare, for instance, Wirth, *Türkei und Persien*, and idem, *Geschichte der Türken* (Stuttgart: Franck'sche Verlagsbuchhandlung, 1912). Wirth was one of the most radical warmongers of the Pan-German League. In this context he actively advocated German-Ottoman cooperation. Michael Peters, *Der Alldeutsche Verband am Vorabend des Ersten Weltkriegs (1908–1914)* (Frankfurt am Main–Bern: Lang, 1992), pp. 112-13. On the early connection between racism and German imperialism, see Werner Jochmann, "Antisemitismus im Deutschen Kaiserreich 1871-1914," in *Juden im Wilhelminischen Deutschland. Ein Sammelband, Mosser,* ed. E. Werner and Arnold Paucker (Tübingen: Christians, 1976), reprinted as Werner Jochmann, *Gesellschaftskrise und Judenfeindschaft in Deutschland 1870–1945,* Hamburger Beiträge zur Sozial- und Zeitgeschichte, Band 23 (Hamburg, 1988; 2d ed. 1991), p. 66.

voked the massacres by "sucking the blood" of the Muslim peasantry.[31]

While Wirth's allegations echoed the established stereotypes on Armenians, he did add an important aspect: He nominated himself as champion of the Kurds. He described Kurds as "a splendid race"—fresh, brave, frank, and trusting—just as Tacitus had described the ancient Germans. Alleging that Muslim peasants in the Ottoman Empire and German colonists in the Caucasus were exploited by Armenians, Wirth developed the theory that for hundreds of years Armenians had oppressed Kurds and that only quite recently had the latter taken revenge. Wirth reported that Germans living in Constantinople viewed the 1896 massacre as a lesson to Armenians which, however, had been insufficient. Like Naumann, Wirth introduced anonymous experts who made the most extreme statements. To preempt any criticism of his assertions, the author added that not all Armenians were as bad as those described.[32] Wirth's caveats also fulfilled a basic requirement for his racial theories: Since Armenians were considered to be of "Aryan blood," they necessarily could not be completely corrupted. For Wirth, the problem was that Armenian blood had become "thin"; Kurdish blood, however, still had the desirable qualities, and a great Kurdish future was to be hoped for. Thus, Wirth presented the Kurds as the ideal "Aryan" ally Germans might desire in the Near East.[33]

31. Wirth, *Türkei und Persien,* pp. 10, 17, 19, 35, 51.

32. Ibid., pp. 17-18, 19–21, 51. Wirth republished this text in expanded form in idem, *Vorderasien und Ägypten in historischer und politischer, kultureller und wirtschaftlicher Hinsicht geschildert* (Stuttgart: Union Deutsche Verlagsgesellschaft, 1916), pp. 143–54. In this instance Wirth quotes a German journalist who presented his accusations against Armenians by quoting a missionary. The missionary spoke in disapproving terms of Armenians' hopeless lack of honor, honesty, and loyalty. Quoting Ewald Banse and another journalist, Wirth hinted at the feared Armenian-British cooperation; see p. 151-52.

33. Wirth, *Türkei und Persien,* p. 20. Wirth also informed his readers that a successful crossbreeding of Kurds and Armenians was unlikely. See also Albrecht

EWALD BANSE

In the field of geography it was Ewald Banse who produced a monographic study on the Ottoman Empire and its racial composition. His study combined the descriptive qualities of a travelogue, a hypothesis on the mixing of ancient races and its undesirable outcomes, and evaluations of recent political developments. Banse's assessment of Armenians was a collection of the well-established stereotypes further radicalized.[34] Banse maintained that Germany's imperialist rivals had instigated Armenians to rebel:

> The government could not have an interest in conceding to a hostile people the blessings of economic progress and a more independent position, which due to [the Armenian people's] character would only have accelerated secession and separation. It realized early on that only the ruthless suppression of this noisy minority would benefit the welfare of the state and the Islamic majority of its subjects. It gave the signal for a long and, from the viewpoint of humanity, regrettable series of vexatious suppressions by officials, ruthless action by the military, and bloody robberies by the Kurds. Its sole and, in view of the circumstances, not unjustified principle was that to get the Armenian Question out of the world one had to get the Armenians out of the world.[35]

Wirth, *Türkei, Oesterreich, Deutschland,* Monographien zur Zeitgeschichte, Heft 8 (Stuttgart: Arthur Dolge, 1912).

34. Armenians were, for instance, "troublemakers" and "spongers on the loins of the master races," and they were practicing an "impure form of Christianity." Ewald Banse, *Die Türkei. Eine moderne Geographie,* 3d ed. (Braunscheig: Westermann, 1919), pp. 196–98. The book's first edition appeared 1915. In the volume Banse summed up statements and findings of the prewar years. See also Ewald Banse, *Der arische Orient (Orient III),* Aus Natur und Geisteswelt, Bd. 279 (Leipzig: Teubner, 1910).

35. Ibid.

Thus, Banse ultimately saw Armenians as a political obstacle to the economic progress of Ottoman society. While admitting the fact that atrocities had been committed against Armenians, Banse nevertheless saw an antagonistic relationship between the alleged political designs of Armenians, their physical existence, and the welfare of the Ottoman state. Thus, on the eve of World War I, Banse implied that the destruction of the Ottoman Armenian population was an important precondition for Ottoman Turkish progress.[36]

36. In 1917 Banse legitimized the annihilation of the Armenians as follows: "The Armenians would be an extremely dangerous threat to the Turkish empire, if the empire had not been successfully working for some decades to cut down the rebellious elements of the Armenian population by the sword and by turkification. After all, it is understandable that a state takes action with all possible means against an element of the population which is determined not to collaborate toward the common goal. The part has always to stand aside for the whole. Besides, we are of the opinion that the lachrymose sympathies for the Armenians, which were once exhibited by some sides, are only little founded." Ewald Banse, *Die Türken und wir. Ein kleines Mahn- und Geleitwort an sie und uns* (Weimar: A. Duncker, 1917), p.138.

3
GERMAN STEREOTYPES OF
ARMENIANS AND WORLD WAR I

The material introduced so far shows that by 1914 an almost standardized line of argument on Armenians had been developed by authors who concerned themselves with German economic expansion in the Ottoman Empire. Anti-Armenian views held in common united writers of the extreme anti-Semitic right and national-liberals. It was the latter group, however, that would have a determining impact on German Middle East propaganda during World War I.

ERNST JÄCKH

In 1914, the German public enthusiastically welcomed the German-Ottoman military alliance. A wave of propaganda pamphlets further popularized the alliance. Anticipated German gains in the Ottoman Empire, however, were a topic which troubled the German Foreign Office. In this situation, the well-known advocate of a German-Ottoman alliance, Ernst Jäckh, secured a central position within German Middle-East propaganda for himself and his brainchild, the Deutsch-Türkische Vereinigung (German-Turkish Association).[37]

37. On the Deutsch-Türkische Vereinigung, see Jürgen Kloosterhuis, *Friedliche Imperialisten. Deutsche Auslandsvereine und auswärtige Kulturpolitik, 1906-1918,*

The association had been founded on 11 February 1914. It was perhaps the most prestigious of the contemporary German associations concerned with German propaganda abroad. Its membership included scholars, journalist, officers, and representatives of German companies such as the Deutsche Bank, the Orient Bank, and the Anatolian Railway Company. Most of these companies were active in the Ottoman Empire. Significantly, it was Gottlieb von Jagow, the state secretary, who had invited the participants to the constituent assembly, over which he personally presided. Not surprisingly, the German Foreign Office played a role in the formulation of the society's bylaws and its program.[38]

Officially, the new society was set up to discreetly promote German cultural interests in the Ottoman Empire. The founding of German schools and the spread of the German language were prominent tasks. These activities had to be coordinated with the German Foreign Office; financing was secured by the donations of German industrialists and the Foreign Office. Thus, the Foreign Office created a tool to perform undertakings for which its budget, which had to be approved by the parliament after debate, did not make provisions. In other words, the association was able to perform tasks for the Foreign Office which were beyond the control of the parliament.[39]

The strong representation of leading German businesspeople in the association's management suggests that the official statement of purpose did not fully reflect the interests of the member-

---

Europäische Hochschulschriften, Reihe III, Bd. 588 (Frankfurt am Main: Lang, 1994), pp. 595–657. For Jäckh's perception of Ottoman-German relations and his own role see Ernst Jäckh, *Der aufsteigende Halbmond. Auf dem Weg zum deutsch-türkischen Bündnis,* 4th rev. ed. (Stuttgart-Berlin: Deutsche Verlags-Anstalt, 1915), and idem, *Der Goldene Pflug. Lebensernte eines Weltbürgers* (Stuttgart: Deutsche Verlags-Anstalt, 1954).

38. Kloosterhuis, *Friedliche Imperialisten,* p. 602.

39. Ibid., pp. 603–11.

ship. The association did not limit itself to the promotion of German cultural interests or to popularizing the German-Turkish military alliance. Soon, it had developed activities to promote German economic interests in the Ottoman Empire. To systematize these activities, the association established a bureau for information on 1 October 1915 in Berlin, the Auskunftsstelle für deutsch-türkische Wirtschaftsfragen—Deutsch-türkische Wirtschaftszentrale (Information Office for German-Turkish Economic Issues German-Turkish Economic Center). A year later, the bureau was reorganized and renamed Zentral-Geschäftsstelle für deutsch-türkische Wirtschaftsfragen (Central Office for German-Turkish Economic Issues). The director of the institute was Jäckh.[40]

The reorganization of the economic activities of the German-Turkish association brought about an extension in its program and an increase of its influence. The Central Office served a wide audience. Its principal object was to combine scholarly research on the Ottoman Empire with practical activities by German businesspeople. To achieve this, the office started to issue a number of publications on topics such as Ottoman tariffs, laws, and mining, that were of immediate interest to German business-people. Moreover, the office published a journal, *Archiv für Wirtschaftsforschung im Orient* (Archive for economic research in the Orient).

The Central Office advocated the strengthening of the Ottoman economy, arguing that Ottoman economic expansion would benefit German-Ottoman trade. From this perspective, German investments were seen as supporting the political and economic designs of the ruling Ottoman Committee of Union and Progress (CUP). The Central Office's wish to emphasize that

40. Ibid., pp. 661–78. Lothar Rathmann, *Stossrichtung Nahost 1914-1918. Zur Expansionspolitik des deutschen Imperialismus im ersten Weltkrieg* (Berlin: Rütten & Loening, 1963), pp. 147–50.

German and Ottoman economic interests were in harmony with each other was important since CUP circles feared German attempts to take over control of the Ottoman economy.[41] Such fears were nurtured in part by intensified German Middle-East propaganda and occasional imperialistic comments by German officers while on duty in the Middle East. As a result, *Archiv* set out to review German publications on the Ottoman Empire. The Central Office not only criticized undesirable views on the Ottoman ally, but also lobbied for increased censorship of all material to be published on the Ottoman Empire. From 1916 onward, the office participated in the surveillance of the German press. Thus, it had established itself as a prominent institute for the promotion of German economic interests in the Ottoman Empire and had gained a measure of control over potential rival institutions. Now, it was in a position to formulate authoritative views on German-Ottoman relations.[42]

The tasks of the Central Office staff, however, went beyond propaganda and censorship. Jäckh, who since 1908 had established excellent contacts with the CUP leadership, was entrusted with intelligence work. He visited the Ottoman Empire and submitted reports on conditions there. Moreover, he played a role in attempts to silence German Protestants who denounced the Armenian Genocide. Jäckh first used persuasion, and when this failed, called for active repression.[43]

41. Kloosterhuis, *Friedliche Imperialisten,* p. 665; see also Ulrich Trumpener, *Germany and the Ottoman Empire, 1914–1918* (Princeton: Princeton Univ. Press, 1968; reprint, Delmar, N. Y.: Caravan Books, 1989), pp. 317-18.

42. Trumpener, *Germany and the Ottoman Empire,* p. 319. The works of Wirth and Banse, quoted above, give some insight into the kind of material which received the approval of German censorship. Rathmann, *Stossrichtung Nahost,* p. 152.

43. Kloosterhuis, *Friedliche Imperialisten,* pp. 618, 668; Jäckh (Deutsch-Türkische Vereinigung) to Rosenberg (Auswärtiges Amt), Berlin, 24 Aug. 1916, A 22639 Auswärtiges Amt—Politisches Archiv Türkei 183/44; see also Walter Mogk, *Paul Rohrbach und das "Größere Deutschland." Ethischer Imperialismus im Wilhelmi-*

ERNST MARRÉ

As noted, the aims of the scholarly proponents of Ottoman-German cooperation were not simply academic, and their efforts to direct German public opinion according to German foreign policy objectives brought about the desired results. In a pamphlet published in 1916 by Ernst Marré, president of the Turkish association of Leipzig, the author suggested a "practical economic program."[44]

Marré's argument reflected prevalent German concerns. Like the Central Office for German-Turkish Economic Issues, he warned his audience that mistaken views on the Ottoman Empire still existed, and he maintained that a successful "Orient" policy required unbiased and correct information.[45] Marré gave voice to German anxieties about the CUP's drive to nationalize the Ottoman economy.[46] Although he maintained that the CUP's nationalism was as exaggerated as that of the Pan-German League, he agreed that the non-Turkish Ottoman population had to be "turkified." It was in this context that Marré dealt with Ottoman Armenians. He maintained that the Armenian Ques-

---

nischen Zeitalter. Ein Beitrag zur Geschichte des Kulturprotestantismus (Munich: Goldmann, 1972), p. 170.

44. Ernst Marré, *Die Türken und Wir nach dem Kriege. Ein praktisches Wirtschaftsprogramm*, Kriegspolitische Einzelschriften, Heft 11 (Berlin: Schwetschke & Sohn, 1916).

45. Ibid., p. 4.

46. Leading German businessmen like Arthur von Gwinner, director of the Deutsche Bank, were deeply concerned about the losses their companies had to sustain in the Ottoman Empire because of the Armenian Genocide. The head of the Anatolian Railway Company, Franz J. Günther, had informed Gwinner of the Ottoman law of the so-called abandoned properties, commenting that the law might be summarized in two points: "Art. 1) Tous les biens des arméniens sont confisqués. Art. 2) Le Gouvernement encaissera les créances des exilés et il remboursera (ou ne remboursera pas) leurs dettes." Gwinner to Auswärtiges Amt, Berlin, 7 Oct. 1915, A 29127, Auswärtiges Amt—Politisches Archiv Türkei 183/39.

tion was the product of British provocations aimed at harming German trade. The British were not, however, the only allies of Armenians, according to Marré. Marré accused Armenians of having russified various Ottoman regions, thus posing a threat to the Ottoman government's war effort; the Ottoman government had consequently been forced to remove them. In Marré's view, German businesspeople would benefit in the future from the deportation of the Armenian population, since Armenians had been a danger to German enterprise. Like his predecessors of the prewar period, Marré blamed Armenians for their lack of character. Only their cowardice, according to Marré, prevented Armenians from dealing with stolen goods and theft. The Armenians, Marré claimed, regarded open cheating to be "business" and, taking up Körte's old cliché, Marré alleged that cheating had become a sport for Armenians.[47]

EUGEN MITTWOCH

During World War I Eugen Mittwoch, an orientalist originally teaching at the seminar for Oriental languages in Berlin, was active in the Foreign Office's Nachrichtenstelle für den Orient (Information Center for the Orient).[48] He wrote and edited propaganda material intended, for instance, to popularize the idea of a Muslim "holy war" against the Entente in Germany and abroad.[49] Mittwoch, moreover, took part in efforts to induce

47. Marré, *Die Türken und Wir nach dem Kriege*, pp. 7-8, 9, 11-12, 15, 17, 21, 35.

48. On the Nachrichtenstelle für den Orient see Herbert Landolin Müller, *Islam, gihad ("Heiliger Krieg") und Deutsches Reich. Ein Nachspiel zur wilhelminischen Weltpolitik im Maghreb 1914-1918*, Europäische Hochschulschriften, Reihe III, Bd.506 (Frankfurt am Main: Lang, 1991), pp. 193–233; Kloosterhuis, *Friedliche Imperialisten*, pp.439–42.

49. Eugen Mittwoch, *Deutschland, die Türkei und der Heilige Krieg*, Kriegsschriften des Kaiser-Wilhelm-Dank Vereins der Soldatenfreunde, Heft 17 (Berlin: Kameradschaft, 1914). For a recently published collection of materials from the Information Center, see Gottfried Hagen, *Die Türkei im Ersten Weltkrieg. Flugblät-*

Muslim prisoners of war in Germany to join the Ottoman army. At times he was also charged with intelligence missions to Switzerland.

While the dissemination of German propaganda on behalf of the Ottoman ally was a central task of the Information Center, the control and suppression of undesirable public activities in Germany was another. Thus Mittwoch reported on the Armenian community in Berlin and on those Germans who cooperated with Armenians in the effort to make the Armenian Genocide known in Germany.[50]

In 1916 Mittwoch published a study in the *Archiv für Wirtschaftsforschung im Orient* on "The Economic Importance of the Language Question in Turkey."[51] The author argued that in the Ottoman Empire languages were distributed spatially according to the settlement areas of the various nationalities and socially according to the position certain ethnic groups had obtained within the economy. Thus, in order to be economically successful, foreigners had to know more than one language spoken in the Ottoman Empire.[52] As most of the western businesspeople did not have the necessary knowledge, they were forced to hire local interpreters. According to Mittwoch, these interpreters more than once managed to take over the business from the Europeans and to establish themselves as intermediaries in the

ter und Flugschriften in arabischer, persischer und osmanisch-türkischer Sprache aus einer Sammlung der Universitätsbibliothek Heidelberg. Eingeleitet, übersetzt und kommentiert, Heidelberger orientalistische Studien, Bd.15 (Frankfurt am Main: Lang, 1990).

50. Wesendonk, Berlin, 8 June 1915, A 18243 Auswärtiges Amt—Politisches Archiv Türkei 183/37; Wesendonk, Berlin, 18 June, A 19225 AA-PA Türkei 183/37; Wesendonk, Berlin, 14 Aug. 1915; marginal note from Mittwoch to Wesendonk, Berlin, 19 Aug. 1915, A 23552 AA-PA Deutschland 126g adh. 1/1.

51. Eugen Mittwoch, "Die wirtschaftliche Bedeutung der Sprachenfrage in der Türkei," *Archiv für Wirtschaftsforschung im Orient* 1 (1916), pp. 317–43.

52. Ibid., p. 324.

trade.[53] Recently, however, the situation had changed profoundly. In Mittwoch's view, this was not due to the deportation of the Armenians, but because of the new language law, which made the use of Turkish in all business transactions obligatory. Mittwoch noted that foreign companies would have to face numerous temporary problems such as a change in staff. He avoided mentioning the political background for the new law.[54] Mittwoch argued that in the end the change would benefit German businesspeople because it homogenized economic life and thus simplified matters.[55]

Mittwoch tried to promote the Turkish-language policy. The policy of eliminating Armenian businesspeople and employees was an integral part of the Armenian Genocide. The application of the language law was directly linked to the attempted or actual deportation and ensuing massacre of those Armenians who were meant to be removed or were actually removed. Concerned about the repercussions of the law, German business circles determinedly protested against it. Thus, Mittwoch opposed exactly those interests which the *Archiv* was supposed to further.

Mittwoch's article was an instance of German propagandistic support for the genocidal policies of Germany's Ottoman ally. Further, the author broadened the concept of an ethnic division of labor, maintaining that this division had resulted in a linguistic division of labor as well. In presenting this situation as a complicated language problem, Mittwoch not only speculated on the economic benefits of the Armenian Genocide for future German investors, but also constructed, at least implicitly, a community

53. Mittwoch also compared the situation with that in other countries. It is interesting to note that he uses the term "Komprador," which, as we will see, was to play a key role in the framework of dependency theory. Ibid., p. 336.

54. Ibid., pp. 337–40.

55. Ibid., pp. 342 ff.

of German and Ottoman interests in exterminating the Ottoman Armenians.

ALPHONS SUSSNITZKI

The theme of the turkification of the Ottoman economy was taken up in more comprehensive manner by the journalist Alphons Sussnitzki. His article "Zur Gliederung wirtschaftlicher Arbeit nach Nationalitäten in der Türkei" (On the division of labor according to nationality in Turkey) appeared in *Archiv für Wirtschaftsforschung im Orient* in 1917.[56]

Discussing the pre–World War I structure of the Ottoman economy, Sussnitzki maintained that, by and large, professions were each dominated by members of one racial group.[57] This thesis was not an original contribution; a number of authors writing on the Ottoman Empire had popularized the impression of a preponderance of ethnic minorities in parts of the economy. Such views were developed into a more coherent thesis by Eugen Mittwoch and Siegfried Lichtenstädter. Lichtenstädter had argued that economic specialization was not racially transmitted but was a social phenomenon. According to him, less powerful groups had been forced out of agriculture and became prominent in commerce and industry; in following their own interests they furthered the overall economy. Lichtenstädter presented the role of minority groups in a very positive light.[58] He explicitly rejected the idea that Armenians were economically responsible

---

56. Alphons J. Sussnitzki, "Zur Gliederung wirtschaftlicher Arbeit nach Nationalitäten in der Türkei," *Archiv für Wirtschaftsforschung im Orient* 2 (1917), pp. 382–407. The author was a journalist who between 1911 and 1918 reported for several German newspapers on Ottoman affairs. Contributing to the *Allgemeine Zeitung des Judentums,* he reported on the affairs of the Ottoman Jewish community and the Zionist movement. In 1918 his articles appeared in the *Weltwirtschaftszeitung,* where he discussed problems of the Ottoman economy.

57. Ibid., p. 382.

58. Siegfried Lichtenstädter, "Nationalität, Religion und Berufsgliederung im Oriente," *Beiträge zur Kenntnis des Orients* 8 (1910), pp. 56, 67.

for their own massacres and that Armenians were "bloodsuckers." Quite the contrary, he argued, an ethnic division of labor would have socially stabilizing effects, and, accordingly, the worst bloodshed had occurred in places where this division was not fully established.[59] Moreover, the author concluded that with the further abandonment of agriculture by Armenians, an Armenian national renaissance and an independent Armenian state became less likely. Lichtenstädter suggested that the ethnic division of labor was not the cause of social tensions but a way out of political antagonisms.[60]

It was, however, the work of Sussnitzki that had the greatest impact on future academic writing. Sussnitzki considered the role of Turks, Greeks, Armenians, and Jews in three sectors of the economy: agriculture, crafts and industry (*Gewerbe*), and trade.

In agriculture, a major difference between Turks, on the one hand, and Greeks and Armenians, on the other, according to Sussnitzki, was the selection of the crops they grew. Turks were characterized as more passive and only slowly switching from subsistence production to commercial agriculture. Greeks and Armenians, however, were said to prefer cash crops, as they lacked a deep connection to the soil on which they worked.

In industry and crafts, Sussnitzki claimed, the various ethnic communities reserved a number of professions to themselves. Although they all did this, he added, certain racial characteristics could be identified. For instance, Turks distinguished themselves in the making of carpets, as they were psychologically especially well-disposed for this work.

The most important and glaring differences existed, according to Sussnitzki, within Ottoman trade. He claimed that Greeks and Armenians controlled nearly all trade, and profiting from a wide spatial distribution of their communities, these two groups had

59. Ibid, pp. 68–69.
60. Ibid., p. 70.

obstructed the development of other nationalities. Sussnitzki argued that usury and the exploitation of foreign protection further contributed to the economic ascendancy of these groups.[61] Sussnitzki reported that according to a popular saying, a Greek could swindle two Jews, whereas an Armenian could swindle two Greeks. For Sussnitzki, the main cause for the minorities' importance lay elsewhere, however. Sussnitzki wrote: "These external circumstances, together with the above-mentioned certainly preponderant racial characteristic, fully explain the total insignificance of Turks in trade, as we actually encounter it."[62]

Concluding his overview, the author claimed that Armenians had abused Ottoman Turkish tolerance and their own position as intermediaries in the Ottoman economy. Yet, he warned, because of the existing division of labor, it would be damaging to the CUP's interests if Armenians were excluded from the Ottoman economy at once. He noted that given the nationalist policy of the CUP, this issue was of prime importance. Sussnitzki stated that the exclusion of Armenians and Greeks was nevertheless necessary, as they were under British and French influence and would always work for the interests of the Entente powers. To substitute for Armenians and Greeks, Sussnitzki proposed supporting Ottoman Jews, Arabs, and *dönmes* (converts to Islam), since Turks lacked the racial aptitude for trade—unless they were Turks from Crete, of Greek racial origin. He concluded that the Ottoman Empire lacked competent human resources and the nationalization of the Turkish economy and its future development would require cooperation with foreigners. In sum, given

61. Sussnitzki, "Zur Gliederung wirtschaftlicher Arbeit nach Nationalitäten in der Türkei," p. 396-97.

62. Ibid., p. 401: "Die äußeren Umstände erst zusammen mit der freilich überwiegenden erwähnten völkischen Eigenart erklären völlig die Geringfügigkeit der Bedeutung der Türken im Handel, wie wir sie tatsächlich vorfinden."

the structural problems, Sussnitzki advised an "evolutionary" instead of a "revolutionary" strategy.[63]

Sussnitzki's analysis integrated a number of the familiar stereotypes: that Armenians were the political allies of Germany's enemies and that they played a negative role within the Ottoman economy. Thus the author stressed a basic convergence of Ottoman Turkish and German interests. Indeed, the success of the CUP's turkification program would to some extent depend on German cooperation and aid. In order to recommend increased German economic involvement, the writer had to attribute the alleged negative economic role played by Christian communities to racial characteristics, thus allowing himself to argue that foreign penetration did not necessarily bring about the conditions which the CUP wished to change. In other words, Sussnitzki implied that German-Turkish cooperation would bring about different outcomes than French-Armenian or British-Armenian collaboration. To reach his conclusion Sussnitzki had to build up a racist argument for which he could draw on the stock of German "Orient" propaganda of the prewar period. Pointing out the Ottoman Turkish need for German aid, he encouraged the CUP not to damage German interests. Numerous German companies had had to sustain losses due to the Armenian Genocide as their former customers and partners suddenly disappeared, leaving behind open accounts. However, there was another side to this situation: the mass murder of Armenians had opened up new opportunities for German trade and investment. In this sense, Sussnitzki's article was a calculation of potential German benefits from the Armenian Genocide. It was, as such, German World War I propaganda addressed to both Ottoman and German audiences.

63. Ibid., pp. 405–7.

4

THE REVIVAL OF SUSSNITZKI'S THESIS IN MODERN SCHOLARSHIP

In 1918, after the German defeat and the end of World War I, German plans for a bright future of German trade and investment in the Ottoman Empire came to an end. The German government now had other concerns. Anti-Armenian statements were out of place, as the victorious Entente powers suspected the German government of having played a part in the Armenian Genocide. However, German racist stereotyping of Armenians and accusations of Armenian treason against Ottoman Turks continued. Public statements by German army officers who had served in the Ottoman Army during the war and their memoirs often contained passages seething with hatred against Armenians. These expressions were in part motivated by the desire to exonerate the writers from guilt in the Genocide, as German officers were also suspected of having played a part in the destruction of Ottoman Armenians.[64] In German academia, also, the ethnic

---

64. See, for instance, Hans von Kiesling, *Vorderasien-Rußland Südamerika. Deutsche Auswanderungsgebiet der Zukunft. Auf Grund persönlicher Erfahrungen zusammengestellt* (Leipzig: Dietrische Verlagsbuchhandlung, 1920), pp. 12, 16; and idem, *Orientfahrten. Zwischen Ägeis und Zagros. Erlebtes und Erschautes aus schwerer Zeit* (Leipzig: Dietrische Verlagsbuchhandlung, 1921), p. 7. The accusations of officers like Kiesling found their way also into the studies of military historians who had themselves fought in the Middle East. Carl Mühlmann, *Das deutsch-türkische*

stereotyping of Armenians was kept alive and the concept of a racial division of labor involving Armenians was further developed. For example, in a thesis on Armenians and Kurds published in 1935, the author identified Armenians as parasites.[65] The German defeat in 1945, however, broke the hegemony of racist thought in academia and public circles. Thereafter, racist writings on Armenians could no longer be sustained as scholarship.

CHARLES ISSAWI, WALT ROSTOW, AND MODERNIZATION THEORY

The end of Nazism, the most radical manifestation of ethnic stereotyping and racist thought and politics in German society, did not lead to a disappearance of the existing published material. In 1966, ethnic stereotyping based on such earlier German publications found its way back into scholarship on the Ottoman Empire, this time outside Germany. A collection of materials on the economic history of the Middle East, edited by Charles Issawi, included a translation of Sussnitzki's article. Thus, the thesis of an Ottoman division of labor based on race was presented to a readership that had not until then had access to the German text. Taken out of the political context of German war

---

Waffenbündnis im Weltkrieg. Mit einem Gleitwort von W. Foerster (Leipzig: Köhler & Amelang, 1940), pp. 276-77. Gleich, who like Kiesling had served in a leading position on the Mesopotamian front, was, after having witnessed the Armenian Genocide on his way through Deir ez-Zor, highly critical of German propaganda: "Even if the Armenians had really been swindlers and deceivers as they were presented by our Turk-friendly propaganda, such base acts were scandalous." Gerold von Gleich, *Vom Balkan nach Bagdad. Militärisch-politische Erinnerungen an den Orient* (Berlin: Scherl, 1921), p. 91.

65. Helmut Christoff, "Kurden und Armenier. Eine Untersuchung über die Abhängigkeit ihrer Lebensführung und Charakterentwicklung von der Landschaft" (Ph.D. diss., Hamburg, 1935).

propaganda, the article gave the impression that Sussnitzki was an informed and honest contemporary observer.[66]

The publication of the article by Issawi, himself an advocate of the so-called modernization theory, may have been brought about by similarities between Sussnitzki's thesis and the modernization approach in Ottoman historiography. In fact, the economic concepts proposed by the Central Office for German-Turkish Economic Issues and *Archiv für Wirtschaftsforschung im Orient* during World War I had anticipated several main assumptions of modernization theory. Both views assumed an inherent dichotomy between an actively modernizing core and a reacting society which followed the course of the core. Progress achieved by traditional societies was measured by the degree to which they resembled the socioeconomic structures of the modernizing core. Moreover, both concepts had similar origins: they were developed out of foreign-policy needs. Specifically, they both emerged from a need for a scholarly thesis on the benefits of the subordinate integration of the heavily state-controlled Ottoman or Turkish economy into the system of a superior partner. Thus, Sussnitzki's article could be interpreted as a confirmation of the arguments presented by the modernization approach.[67]

Authors who employed modernization theory maintained that their studies provided an alternative to concepts informed by Marxist theory. Thus they represented a Western ideological answer to a perceived Soviet challenge. A good exponent of this tradition, Walt Rostow, went so far as to call communism a "disease of the transition." While denouncing theories of non-capitalist socioeconomic development on the one hand, Rostow

66. Charles Issawi, ed., *The Economic History of the Middle East, 1800–1914: A Book of Readings* (Chicago: Univ. of Chicago Press, 1966), pp. 115–25.

67. Issawi maintained that what "has been so aptly called ethnic division of labor has characterized the Middle East for centuries, and even millenniums." Ibid., p. 114.

offered precise predictions for the economic growth of a number of countries on the other. According to this prediction, the modern Turkish state should have witnessed an economic "take-off" by 1959.[68]

Issawi's own works reveal the impact of Sussnitzki's thesis. Issawi stressed the importance of minorities in the socioeconomic transformation of the Middle East. Various factors were held responsible for the success of principally Christian groups. These Christian circles were said to have enjoyed a better education than Muslims and to have profited from foreign protection and legal reforms in the Ottoman Empire. Moreover, they were said to have possessed a high degree of group solidarity which allowed them to control important segments of the economy.[69] However, the successful contribution by minorities to the economic transformation of certain areas allegedly also functioned as an impediment to further progress, since, according to Issawi, "there was the feeling in government circles that industrial development would be carried out mainly by, and for the benefit of, foreigners or members of minority groups, which considerably diminished its attraction."[70]

This interpretation was further expanded by an assessment of the make-up of minority groups. Again, reviewing the policies of

68. Walt Whitman Rostow, *The Stages of Economic Growth. A Non-communist Manifesto*, 2d. ed. (Cambridge: Cambridge Univ. Press, 1971), pp. xx, 162–64; Cyril Edwin Black, *The Dynamics of Modernization: A Study in Comparative History* (New York: Harper & Row, 1967); Alexander Gerschenkron, *Economic Backwardness in Historical Perspective: A Book of Essays* (Cambridge: Harvard Univ. Press, 1962). For a critique of the modernization paradigm, see Leonard Binder, "The Natural History of Development Theory," *Comparative Studies in Society and History* 28 (1986), p. 3: "Modernization theory is essentially an academic, and pseudo-scientific, transfer of the dominant, ideologically significant paradigm employed in research on the American political system."

69. Charles Issawi, *An Economic History of the Middle East and North Africa* (New York: Columbia Univ. Press, 1982), p. 89.

70. Ibid., p. 158.

the Ottoman government and post–World War I Middle Eastern governments, Issawi stated that "the fact that the economically most active part of their population consisted of unassimilable minorities, who would presumably be the main beneficiaries of development, must have further reduced their inclination."[71]

The assumption that minorities were "unassimilable" as such echoes the generalizations of Sussnitzki's contemporaries on the "characteristics" of minorities. It reflects the view that society ideally is as nationalists define it. It takes very little to arrive from this view to the inference that Ottoman communities as such were acting in conflict with each other. Ottoman economic success was, according to this view, the cause of its own undoing since the agents of change were the wrong ones.

Issawi wrote: "The feeling of being overwhelmed and driven out caused much resentment among Turks and helps to account for the intense bitterness and violence in the struggle between Turks, Armenians, and Greeks in the period from 1896 to 1923."[72]

Here Issawi echoed the surmise of earlier writers that Armenian economic success provoked violence in the Ottoman Empire. Thus, "economic provocation" was presented as a cause of the Armenian massacres of the 1890s and 1909, the Armenian Genocide, and the expulsion of Greeks from the modern Turkish state in the 1920s. Issawi did away with the distinction between victims and aggressors. The perpetrators of massacres and genocide, and the state itself, became the underdogs in a "struggle" for what was rightfully theirs.

71. Ibid., pp. 177–78. One may note the resemblance between this and the preceding quote on the one hand and Banse's statement referred to above on the other.

72. Charles Issawi, *The Economic History of Turkey, 1800–1914* (Chicago: Univ. of Chicago Press, 1980), p. 56.

DEPENDENCY THEORY

During the 1960s, the ideological bias and dichotomous character of modernization theory came under attack. By this time, the promise of instant social and economic benefits for countries that chose to follow the Western example had been proved wrong. Moreover, the idea of western-style democratization had lost much of its appeal in view of the total war the United States waged on the People's Republic of Vietnam.

A scholarly formulation of the growing uneasiness with modernization theory was dependency theory. This theory provided a negative assessment of the impact of western penetration on social and economic structures in the Middle East.[73] Like the modernization approach, dependency theory distinguished between two poles in the world economy: a core area and undeveloped regions. The core integrated a peripheral area by subordinating it through socioeconomic penetration. Thus, the periphery remained a supplier of raw materials, receiving in exchange the finished products of the core. Controlling trade, the core prevented the development of an industrial base in the periphery.

In the process of subordination, some local elites which dissociated themselves and their interests from the rest of the population were co-opted by the core. This group, known as "compradors" in dependency terminology, served as local agents of the core's interests. Thus, dependency prevented the development of a self-aware bourgeoisie in the periphery.

During the 1970s, dependency theory gained influence in research on the Ottoman Empire. Since this approach might be understood as a critique of imperialism and as a call for national

---

73. See, for instance, Andre Gunder Frank, *Capitalism and Underdevelopment in Latin America: Historical Studies of Chile and Brazil*, 4th ed. (New York and London: Modern Reader, 1969).

economic development, it lent itself well to interpretations within nationalist as well as class-oriented concepts of Ottoman history. Furthermore, the adoption of dependency theory by researchers was facilitated by the existence of an early predecessor in the 1930s which resembled the theory in some of its elements.[74] Moreover, dependency theory's construction of a "comprador class" allowed governing views on minorities and their negative impact on Ottoman economic development to be maintained or reformulated.

DOĞU ERGIL AND STEPHEN TED ROSENTHAL

The fusion of the concepts of anti-imperialism and national economic development is illustrated in the work of Doğu Ergil. He interpreted the anti-Armenian policy of the CUP as an anti-colonial struggle against Western imperialism and domestic comprador capitalist classes.[75] Thus, the Armenian bourgeoisie was viewed as an alien factor within the Ottoman socioeconomic structure. Stephen Ted Rosenthal also wrote in detail of the alienated and the foreign-determined nature of the non-Muslim Ottoman bourgeoisie. He examined the category of "cultural

74. On the so-called "Kadro" school see Fikret Adanır, "Zur 'Etatismus'-Diskussion in der Türkei in der Weltwirtschaftskrise. Die Zeitschrift Kadro 1932–1934," in *Der Nahe Osten in der Zwischenkriegszeit. Die Interdependenz von Politik, Wirtschafts und Ideologie,* ed. Linda Schatkowski Schilcher and Claus Scharf (Stuttgart: Steiner, 1989), pp. 355–73; Giacomo E. Carretto, "Polemiche fra kemalismo, fascismo, comunismo, negli anni '30," *Storia Contemporanea* 8 (1977), pp. 489–530; Haldun Gülalp, "Nationalism, Statism and the Turkish Revolution: An Early 'Dependency' Theory," *Review of Middle East Studies* 4 (1988), pp. 69–85; İlhan Tekeli and Selim İlkin, "Türkiye'de bir Aydın," *Toplum ve Bilim* 24 (1984), pp. 35–67.

75. Doğu Ergil, "A Reassessment: The Young Turks, their Politics and Anti-Colonial Struggle," *Balkan Studies* 16 (1975), p. 28; see also, Doğu Ergil and Robert I. Rhodes, "Western Capitalism and the Disintegration of the Ottoman Empire: The Impact of the World Capitalist System on Ottoman Society," *Economy and History* 18 (1975), pp. 41–60.

dependency," and argued that the "clientele class" obtained its cultural values and patterns of consumption from the core and thus did not develop dynamically.[76]

Rosenthal focused on nineteenth-century urban reform in Constantinople: The Ottoman government entrusted the local non-Muslim elite with the organization of a model municipal administration. However, the leading merchants took up the opportunity to promote their own interests. Their principal projects and innovations were to develop facilities for trade and the building of a town hall. Enjoying the tax-free status of protégés of European states, the local elite refused to carry its share of the financial burden it had itself created. Moreover, the merchants did not view the political concessions the Ottoman state had granted them as an occasion to identify themselves more strongly with the Ottoman bureaucracy. Instead, their newly gained competences were used to increase the merchants' power against the Ottoman state.

Rosenthal summarized the results of this strategy as follows:

> The foundation of the municipality of Galata provided the opportunity for the non-Muslim bourgeois to extend their private patterns of consumption of European culture to the areas of public works and administration without regard for the benefits to the rest of the population.[77]

According to Rosenthal, the unsatisfactory performance of non-Muslims led the Ottoman state to reconsider the municipal reform plan and put Muslim state administrators in the merchants' place. Rosenthal added that the officials displayed the desired sense of communal responsibility and took care that the benefits of municipal reform were enjoyed by a larger segment of

---

76. Stephen Ted Rosenthal, *The Politics of Dependency: Urban Reform in Istanbul,* Contributions in Comparative Colonial Studies, no. 3 (Westport, Conn.: Greenwood Press, 1980), pp .xxi-xxii.

77. Ibid., p. xxvi.

the local population. Rosenthal concluded that Muslim administrators were relatively successful because they "were not handicapped by the same degree of cultural dependence as their non-Muslim predecessors."[78]

The underlying logic of Rosenthal's argument is an acceptance of the Ottoman state's paternalistic point of view. A different interpretation could stress that the local non-Muslim elite simply refused to interpret its own role in the terms of the Ottoman state, that it showed a remarkable degree of self-awareness and pursued its own projects utilizing any political support it could muster. Thus, the construction of a visible and distinguished symbol of bourgeois power, the new town hall, formed a primary concern for the community leaders. The neglect of the interests of the district's poor in favor of projects serving the merchants' immediate economic activities points to the existence of a class with its own identity, an identity that did not include concepts of communal welfare based on either Muslim, Christian, or Jewish principles.

In sum, Rosenthal's study illustrates a problematic element in the interpretation of the dependency approach within Ottoman studies: the projects of social classes are assessed with respect to the patterns of interstate relations, the perspectives of local bourgeoisies are neglected, and inordinate attention is paid to the political designs of the government. In this context, the presumed foreign determination of a local bourgeoisie and the identification of this bourgeoisie as a comprador class cannot adequately explain the actual projects of this bourgeoisie. Instead, recourse is made to a political or moral argument. Thus, we may argue that nationalist ideology defines who is a comprador and who is not. We will see that the application of dependency theory left enough room to integrate key perspectives furnished by

78. Ibid.

German nationalist writing of the pre–World War I period, including anti-Armenian propaganda materials. Ironically, a theory designed to criticize the modernization approach reproduced the very same stereotypes of Armenians based on the very same flawed material.

FEROZ AHMAD

In a series of studies, Feroz Ahmad discussed the social and economic policies of the CUP between 1908 and 1918.[79] In these studies, the role of non-Muslim minorities received much attention. Ahmad, too, claimed that non-Muslims increasingly dominated the Ottoman economy during the nineteenth century. Discussing the strategies of non-Muslim economic elites, he stressed that these elites had linked their interests with the European powers and had even become citizens of foreign states, thus constituting a comprador class. Ahmad explicitly rejected the premise that the non-Muslim economic elites formed an Ottoman bourgeoisie, since the

> aspirations of the comprador bourgeoisie were better served the more the authority of the Ottoman State was weakened. Thus if we consider a positive relationship between bourgeoisie and State to be a necessary component in defining such a class, we must conclude that a Turkish bourgeoisie did not exist until the Unionists set about creating one. Prior to the revolution of 1908

79. Feroz Ahmad, "Vanguard of a Nascent Bourgeoisie: The Social and Economic Policy of the Young Turks, 1908–1918," in *Social and Economic History of Turkey (1071–1920)*, ed. Osman Okyar and Halil İnalcik (Ankara: Meteksan Limited Şirketi, 1980), pp. 329–50; Feroz Ahmad, "Unionist Relations with the Greek, Armenian, and Jewish Communities of the Ottoman Empire, 1908–1914," in *Christians and Jews in the Ottoman Empire: The Functioning of a Plural Society*, ed. Benjamin Braude and Bernard Lewis, vol. 1 (New York: Holmes & Meier, 1982), pp. 401–43; Feroz Ahmad, "The Agrarian Policy of the Young Turks, 1908–1918," in *Économie et Sociétés dans l' Empire Ottoman (fin du XVIIIᵉ-début du XXᵉ siècle)*, ed. Jean-Louis Bacqué-Grammont and Paul Dumont (Paris: CNRS, 1983), pp. 275–88.

there was no such class amongst the Muslims, and most non-Muslims did not regard the Ottoman State as their state.[80]

Ahmad suggested a harmonious relationship between government and bourgeoisie as the determining element for a native bourgeoisie—a construct which required a correspondence in the interests and projects of the Ottoman state bureaucracy and economic elites.

Describing the results of the cooperation between the Europeans and the Greek and Armenian minorities, Ahmad subscribed to Sussnitzki's statement of a "division of labor according to nationality."[81] In his use of Sussnitzki's work, however, Ahmad was forced to alter the original thesis in a decisive detail. As shown above, Sussnitzki advocated foreign investment in the Ottoman Empire, presenting such investments in a positive light while attributing negative outcomes of past foreign investments to Armenian racial characteristics. This outline did not pose any fundamental interpretative problem for authors like Issawi who subscribed to the modernization approach, since they, too, had a positive view of foreign investments. However, as dependency theory—with which the thesis of a comprador class is linked—was critical of foreign capital, a fundamental contradiction arose between Sussnitzki's and Ahmad's interpretations. Ahmad solved this problem by turning Sussnitzki's statement upside down. Summing up the German's argument Ahmad wrote:

> Sussnitzki furnishes various reasons for this state of affairs but as a "final cause" puts forward "the protection they enjoyed from foreign powers, whose subjects they sometimes were, thus becoming, thanks to the former Capitulations, exempt from taxation."[82]

80. Ahmad, "Vanguard of a Nascent Bourgeoisie," pp. 329-30; see also Feroz Ahmad, *The Making of Modern Turkey,* The Making of the Middle East Series (London: Routledge, 1993), p. 44.

81. Ahmad, "Vanguard of a Nascent Bourgeoisie," p. 331; idem, "Unionist Relations," p. 405.

82. Ahmad, "Unionist Relations," p. 406.

Thus, Ahmad attributed negative outcomes to Armenians not by reference to their supposed racial characteristics but by identifying them directly with foreign capital.

According to Ahmad, continuing differences between the comprador class and the CUP brought about the CUP's economic nationalization policy. The government was "determined to raise the level of their own social class even at the expense of the minorities and the Ottoman ruling class."[83] The government's policy was a response to the attitudes of the minorities who "had every interest in keeping the Ottoman state weak, though not so weak as to bring about its demise. Such a fine balance could not be maintained indefinitely."[84] Thus, the compradors provoked the reaction by the state and, as in the work of Ergil, Ahmad argues that Armenians could not be an integrated part of the socioeconomic structure. Ahmad expanded his interpretation of the conflict further when he argued that the essentially political struggle between the CUP-controlled governments and the compradors was "rooted in a class conflict" against "all privileged classes."[85] Here, then, the chauvinist policies of the government were explained in Marxist-inspired vocabulary.[86]

83. Ibid., p. 414.

84. Feroz Ahmad, "The Late Ottoman Empire," in *The Great Powers and the End of the Ottoman Empire,* ed. Marian Kent (London: Allen & Unwin, 1984), p. 22.

85. Ahmad, "Unionist Relations," p. 403. On the class basis of the CUP, see Feroz Ahmad, "War and Society Under the Young Turks, 1908–1918," in *Review* 11 (1988), p. 267: "The Unionists, who constituted the most radical wing of the Young Turk movement, represented what may be described as Gramsci's 'subordinate class.' In the late Ottoman Empire, this class had become politically organized and articulate, demanding a place for Ottoman Muslims in the social and economic structure, a constitutional state, and a new intellectual and moral order to go with it."

86. Recently Ahmad has raised the question whether the declared ethnic division of labor impeded the development of class consciousness in Ottoman society. Again, Sussnitzki serves as the evidence: "If, as Sussinitzki tells us, the division of labor in the Ottoman Empire was based largely on ethnic division, then economic

In sum, Ahmad combined the nationalist substance of Sussnitzki's thesis with a theoretical apparatus that was inspired by an anti-imperialist tendency. Moreover, an overtly nationalist rhetoric was translated into vocabulary which exhibited the theoretical influences of Weberian or Marxist class concepts. Dependency theory left enough room to accommodate nationalist notions of social development. It did not lead to a reinterpretation of the role of Ottoman Armenian elites or to the demise of ethnic stereotyping. On the contrary, ethnic stereotyping was introduced into the discourse of allegedly critical scholarship.

WORLD SYSTEM THEORY

During the 1970s, the dependency approach was further developed into the theory of a world system. The modern world system was understood as encompassing a core, a semi-periphery, and a periphery. The relative position of states were not fixed; thus the dependent structure of a peripheral economy might be overcome. The world system approach kept the emphasis on the importance of international trade for the economic development of a society.[87]

---

competition would have led to a greater consciousness based on ethnicity and religion. The social and economic policy of the CUP was designed largely to foster a 'national economy' and to create a 'national bourgeoisie'. That could be accomplished by breaking the hold that the minorities had over the economy which entailed emphasis on the 'national' rather than the social aspects of the struggle, or at least seeing the minorities as the exploiting classes." Feroz Ahmad, "The Development of Class-consciousness in Republican Turkey, 1923–45," in *Workers and the Working Class in the Ottoman Empire and the Turkish Republic, 1839–1950*, ed. Donald Quataert and Erik Jan Zürcher (London and New York: I. B. Taurus, 1995), p. 78.

87. On world system theory see Immanuel Wallerstein, *The Modern World System: Capitalist Agriculture and the Origins of the European World Economy in the Sixteenth Century* (New York: Academic Press, 1974). For a critical comment see Eric R. Wolf, *Europe and the People without History* (Berkeley and Los Angeles: Univ. of California Press, 1982).

REŞAT KASABA

In 1988 Reşat Kasaba published a study on the world-market integration of the Smyrna region during the nineteenth century. According to him, foreign trade was the principal stimulus for the transformation of the Ottoman regional economy. Thus, the author, like dependency theorists before him, emphasized the importance of commercial elites. However, Kasaba did not subscribe to the concept of a comprador bourgeoisie but defined non-Muslim elites more neutrally as "intermediaries" or as a profit-maximizing "genuine bourgeoisie."[88]

Referring to Sussnitzki, Kasaba assumed that from the beginning of the eighteenth century Christian minorities successfully managed to dominate Ottoman trade and became "the main beneficiaries of the expanding relations between the Ottoman Empire and the capitalist world economy." According to Kasaba, using "speculation and profiteering" Greeks managed to expand their relative importance. Crucial in this, however, Kasaba claimed, was the fact that non-Muslim intermediaries engaged in tax farming, thereby diversifying their economic activities and stabilizing their influence. Around 1815, that is "at the end of the period of incorporation, the Ottoman Empire was closer to occupying an intermediate position within the ambit of the world economy than being pushed to its periphery."[89] Kasaba wrote that during the recession following the Napoleonic Wars, it was Greek intermediaries who financed Greek secessionism.[90] He

---

88. Reşat Kasaba, *The Ottoman Empire and the World Economy: The Nineteenth Century,* SUNY Series in Middle Eastern Studies (Albany: SUNY, 1988), p. 114. "But the historical antagonism between the non-Muslim intermediaries and foreign capital and capitalists suggests that the commonly held inferences about the compradore nature of the former are misleading for this period." Reşat Kasaba, "Izmir," *Review* 16 (1993), pp. 406-7.

89. Kasaba, *The Ottoman Empire and the World Economy,* p. 37.

90. Ibid., pp. 28, 29-30, 100.

claimed that it was this political siding of Greek elites during the Greek War of Independence that would later have serious negative consequences.

Kasaba interpreted the developments of the next decades as follows: The Ottoman government tried, given the problems with the Greeks, to secure the allegiance of non-Muslim groups in reforming the empire's legal structure and thereby underwriting the territorial integrity of the state. However, the application of the state's reform program faced numerous problems at the local level.[91] Most important was that non-Muslims rejected the state's efforts to create a homogeneous political entity under the guiding principle of "Ottomanism." Reform meant political centralization of power in the hands of the government. Consequently, it would have brought about the elimination of economic opportunities for non-Muslims, since non-Muslims profited from "disorder and anarchy."[92]

Kasaba, therefore, saw non-Muslim intermediaries as a peripheral bourgeoisie:

> Ceteris paribus, the regulation that the government was trying to impose was anathema to the tax farmers, merchants, and the money-lenders who had prospered in an environment of economic anarchy. Their preference for a weak state and for the continuation of relations with the world economy in a manner that was devoid of organizational and structural stability distinguished these groups as a peripheral bourgeoisie from their counterparts in the core and the semiperipheral areas, who had come to exert more direct influence on their state apparati.[93]

91. Ibid., pp. 52, 67.

92. Ibid., pp. 58-59; Reşat Kasaba, "Was There a Compradore Bourgeoisie in Mid-Nineteenth-Century Western Anatolia?" *Review* 11 (1988) pp. 219-20.

93. Kasaba, *The Ottoman Empire and the World Economy,* p. 60; see also Kasaba, "Izmir," p. 403.

To secure their political and economic privileges, intermediaries acquired foreign passports, thus gaining the tax-free status of non-Ottoman citizens. In doing so, the non-Muslim bourgeoisie overcame an important economic disadvantage in relation to foreign merchants. It was this special status which contributed considerably to their occupying central positions in local banking, trade, and tax farming.[94] Commanding substantial liquid funds the non-Muslims possessed "a distinct advantage over government officials and foreign merchants."[95] Being firmly established in the local economy, the intermediaries opposed governmental attempts at fiscal reorganization and the foreign penetration of the hinterland of Smyrna. Opposition to foreign penetration, however, did not mean that cooperation with European merchants was unthinkable if it was beneficial to the intermediaries' interests.[96]

It was not only foreigners and Ottoman officials who had to reckon with non-Muslims' economic power. Peasant households, too, felt the intermediaries' influence. These households became increasingly dependent on non-Muslim merchants for the financing of their production and the marketing of their crops. This dependence easily led to debts and loss of land. Thus, the nineteenth century saw the rise of intermediaries as landlords and

94. Kasaba, *The Ottoman Empire and the World Economy*, pp. 70-71, 75, 79, 80. "Typically, the intermediary group as a whole had four avenues for generating profit. These were tax farming, money-lending, money-changing, and trade." Kasaba, "Izmir," p. 405.

95. Kasaba, *The Ottoman Empire and the World Economy*, p. 75. Üner Turgay advanced this thesis in arguing that the opposition of non-Muslim merchants to European economic penetration impeded the development of advanced capitalist structures. A. Üner Turgay, "Trade and Merchants in Nineteenth-Century Trabzon: Elements of Ethnic Conflict," in *Christians and Jews in the Ottoman Empire*, p. 302.

96. Kasaba, *The Ottoman Empire and the World Economy*, pp. 83, 100, 113-14; see also Kasaba, "Izmir," p. 404; Kasaba, "Was There a Compradore Bourgeoisie," p. 226.

their entry into commercial agriculture. Generally, the investments of non-Muslim elites in agriculture occurred in boom periods. It was only at these times that the "expected returns justified a diversion of funds from the other venues of easy profit." Therefore, no long-term commitments in trade or investments took place and economic development remained limited. Thus, the "peripheral status of the Ottoman territories was ultimately determined."[97]

The intermediaries' economic success had far-reaching consequences for all segments of Ottoman society, as it took place at the expense of Muslims. The Ottoman bureaucracy and Muslim merchants had to face a decline in their economic wealth and political strength.[98] Members of Muslim elites who suffered were not the only ones to do so however. The cheap finished goods imported by intermediaries undersold Ottoman products and had a negative impact on the manufacturing sector. Muslim artisans who had possessed an important position in the traditional Ottoman ethnic division of labor could not compete any longer. In sum, by "the 1840s the classical system of production and distribution had been replaced by a new social matrix in western Anatolia. A group of mostly non-Muslim 'banker cum merchants' were entrenched in the controlling positions of this matrix."[99]

97. Kasaba, *The Ottoman Empire and the World Economy,* pp. 84-85, 113-14; see also Kasaba "Was There a Compradore Bourgeoisie," p. 222; Kasaba, "Izmir," p. 405.

98. Kasaba, *The Ottoman Empire and the World Economy,* p. 105. "The rise of non-Muslim merchants to wealth and prominence in western Anatolia took place largely at the expense of the predominantly Muslim elite and the Ottoman bureaucracy." Ibid., p. 102.

99. Ibid., p. 105. Referring among other authors to Sussnitzki, Kasaba reproduces the latter's thesis of an ethnic division of labor. Kasaba misrepresents a crucial part of Sussnitzki's thesis, however. While Sussnitzki interpreted this division as the outcome of non-Muslim success, Kasaba maintains that Sussnitzki described a "classical" division of labor which pre-dated the rise of the non-Muslims.

Due to the control of important sectors of the economy by intermediaries, no "longterm organizational or structural stability" could develop. Consequently, the Ottoman Empire was inevitably reduced to a peripheral region of the world economy.[100]

From the 1880s onwards, the organization of the Ottoman economy began to change and the intermediaries had to experience a decline in their economic importance. The establishment of European financial control in the Ottoman Empire in the form of the Ottoman Public Debt Administration critically reduced the influence of intermediaries in the banking sector. Hand in hand with the rise of the Public Debt Administration went a reassertion of bureaucratic centralism. Thus, non-Muslim intermediaries faced simultaneous challenges from two powerful opponents they could not overcome. "The relative isolation of the non-Muslims during the late nineteenth century was also significant politically in that it created the ground for the successful implementation of policies of national enclosure between 1908 and 1923."[101]

In sum, Kasaba rejected the argument that Armenians were compradors since they resisted full penetration. However, Armenian resistance to full penetration allowed some foreign economic penetration and limited Ottoman administrative reform, bringing about negative social, economic, and political consequences similar to those ascribed by dependency theory to the compradors. Kasaba followed Sussnitzki's thesis of a racial division of labor. However, Kasaba's thesis regarding non-Muslim control of trade did not depend on Sussnitzki's work, which was used only as corroborating evidence among other sources.

100. Ibid., p. 105.
101. Ibid., pp. 111-12; Kasaba points out, however, that the success had a high price since the downfall of intermediary influence meant also a defeat for civil society. Ibid., p. 115. See also, Kasaba, "Izmir," pp. 408-9.

Çağlar Keyder

Over the last twenty years Çağlar Keyder has developed an approach to late Ottoman social history which combines elements of the dependency and world system theories with a theory of class. Keyder argued that the class structure of Ottoman society was shaped by the close interrelation between external and internal factors:

> Changes in the structure of external dependency (due to secular and cyclical tendencies in the world-economy) create internal social tension through promoting the development of certain classes or fractions within classes. Such developments lead to conflict between previously dominant and newly rising groups and to novel demands from the political authority by the latter.[102]

The Marxist concept of the Asiatic Mode of Production provided Keyder with a tool to describe the Ottoman bureaucracy as a class in a Marxist sense. Keyder argued as follows: The ruling bureaucracy depended on intermediaries in order to extract the surplus of the peasantry.[103] These intermediaries were mostly non-Muslim merchants who had gained a privileged position through their cooperation with Europeans. Cooperation between non-Muslims and Europeans was instrumental in the economic decline of Muslim merchants who did not enjoy special privileges

---

102. Çağlar Keyder, "Bureaucracy and Bourgeoisie: Reform and Revolution in the Age of Imperialism," *Review* 11 (1988), p. 159.

103. Ibid., p. 160; see also Çağlar Keyder, "The Dissolution of the Asiatic Mode of Production," *Economy and Society* 5 (1976), pp. 178–96; Huri İslamoğlu and Çağlar Keyder, "Agenda for Ottoman History," *Review* 1,1 (1977), pp. 37, 54 (with reference to Sussnitzki); Çağlar Keyder, Y. Eyüp Özveren, and Donald Quataert, "Port Cities in the Ottoman Empire: Some Theoretical and Historical Perspectives," *Review* 16 (1993), p. 524. The idea that the Ottoman bureaucracy constituted a class had been already proposed by Ziya Gökalp, a Turkist politician and writer, who played an important role as a member of the CUP's Central Committee; see Uriel Heyd, *Foundations of Turkish Nationalism: The Life an Teachings of Ziya Gökalp* (London: Luzac, 1950), p. 141.

and were driven out of business.[104] Enjoying their privileges, non-Muslim merchants did not oppose further foreign penetration of the Ottoman economy.[105] Thus, they did not constitute a "national bourgeoisie" but a "comprador class."[106]

The non-Muslims' position and their economic ascendancy brought about a growing polarization between Muslim and Christian populations. This polarization was intensified further as, in some regions, Christian merchants and peasants cooperated because they were "natural allies." Here the author implies that non-Muslim merchants were driven by nationalist considerations to the extent of neglecting their own commercial interests.[107] According to Keyder, national cohesion was further facilitated by the existing "ethnic division of labor" in the Ottoman Empire. Further expanding the contents of Sussnitzki's "classical statement," Keyder assumed that it was this division which "occluded" class struggle and the development of the Ottoman social formation.[108] In another place, however, Keyder assumed

104. Çağlar Keyder, *State & Class in Turkey: A Study in Capitalist Development* (London and New York: Verso, 1987), pp. 21, 32; Çağlar Keyder, *The Definition of Peripheral Economy: Turkey 1923–1929* (Cambridge: Cambridge Univ. Press, 1981), p. 22. "One result of this capitulatory regime was the almost complete disappearance of native merchants to be replaced by Christian minorities carrying the passports of signatory powers. Escaping Ottoman taxation and jurisdiction, merchants of minority origin became middlemen for foreign trading firms which dealt with Turkey." Ibid., p. 8. Keyder implies here that the Christian merchants were not "native"!

105. Keyder, *State & Class in Turkey*, p. 46.

106. Çağlar Keyder, *Emperyalizm-Azgelişmişlik ve Türkiye* (Istanbul: Birikim Yayınları, 1976), pp. 100, 124; see also Çağlar Keyder, "Cumhuriyetin ilk yıllarında Türk tüccarinin 'milli' leşmesi," *Gelişme Dergisi* (1979–1980), p. 239; Çağlar Keyder, "Class and State in the Transformation of Modern Turkey," in *State and Ideology in the Middle East and Pakistan,* ed. Fred Halliday and Hamza Alavi (London: Macmillan, 1988), p. 192; Keyder, *State & Class in Turkey*, p. 22.

107. Keyder, *The Definition of Peripheral Economy*, p. 21.

108. Keyder: "Class and State in the Transformation of Modern Turkey," pp. 192, 200; Keyder, *State & Class in Turkey,* p. 20 n. 21; Keyder, *The Definition of Peripheral Economy*, p. 21.

that the division of labor "evolved into a class differentiation." He claimed that changes in the lifestyle of non-Muslim merchants increased the divide between the Muslim population and Christian merchants further.[109] Consequently, he argued, conditions evolved in which "an economic basis for ethnic conflict" existed.[110]

Keyder contended that the situation became critical for the bureaucratic elites as the compradors opposed bureaucratic attempts at reform. It was this social conflict which "defined the era." According to Keyder, it was of crucial importance that this bureaucracy-bourgeoisie conflict was acted out as a Muslim-Christian ethno-religious conflict due to the "ethnic dislocation" of the bourgeois class. In the end, according to Keyder, both groups failed to transform the Ottoman social formation.[111]

Thus, there would be no compromise between the non-Muslim bourgeoisie and the bureaucracy. The bureaucracy only succeeded in its project by "other means," which Keyder defined as a

109. Çağlar Keyder, "The Agrarian Background and the Origins of the Turkish Bourgeoisie," in *Developmentalism and Beyond: Society and Politics in Egypt and Turkey,* ed. Ayşe Öncü, Çağlar Keyder, and Saad Eddin Ibrahim (Cairo: American Univ. of Cairo Press, 1994), p.50

110. Çağlar Keyder, "The Political Economy of Turkish Democracy," in *Turkey in Transition: New Perspectives,* ed. Irvin C. Schick and Ertuğrul Ahmet Tonak (Oxford: Oxford Univ. Press, 1987), p. 31; Çağlar Keyder, "The Cycle of Sharecropping and the Consolidation of Small Peasant Ownership in Turkey," *Journal of Peasant Studies* 10 (1982/1983), p. 131; Keyder, "The Agrarian Background and the Origins of the Turkish Bourgeoisie," pp. 52, 57.

111. Keyder, "Bureaucracy and Bourgeoisie," pp. 161-62; Keyder, *State & Class in Turkey,* p. 33. "Bureaucratic reformism should be seen as the institutional innovations of a traditional ruling class who cannot fulfill their political project due, on the one hand, to capitulatory privileges and extraterritoriality, and, on the other hand, to nationalist sentiments and irredentist projects of the rising bourgeoisie vented by great power diplomacy." Keyder, "Bureaucracy and Bourgeoisie," pp. 162-63; "Christian merchants, by opposing the legitimacy of the Ottoman state in favour of its dismantling, also relinquished the possibility of a bid for political struggle and primacy through a 'middle class' revolution." Keyder, "Class and State

"bureaucratic reaction against bourgeois ascendancy," a reaction which might also be understood as "a rebellion against the peripheralization of the Ottoman Empire."[112] The reaction manifested itself in a rapid turn of the CUP towards a policy of Turkish nationalism. This change in strategy was motivated by Armenians' opting for the internationalization of the Armenian Question, and Greeks' tending toward "Venizelism."[113] These options resulted in a formidable challenge: "Thus the formation of an intermediary class of Christians coincided with a cultural mission; their co-optation by European business constituted a total project designed to solve the Ottoman problem."[114]

The CUP's answer to the non-Muslim challenge was the nationalization of the economy. This was a process in which the industrial potential of non-Muslims was "wasted," as the new manufacturing sector had "existed almost entirely outside the Moslem population."[115] The nationalization program resulted in a "mass departure, death and exchange of the Christian minori-

---

in the Transformation of Modern Turkey," p. 200.

112. Ibid., p. 163; Keyder, "Class and State in the Transformation of Modern Turkey," p.191.

113. Keyder, "Class and State in the Transformation of Modern Turkey," p.197; see also Çağlar Keyder, "The Dilemma of Cultural Identity on the Margin of Europe," *Review* 16 (1993), p. 20. Earlier, Keyder had argued that the CUP had embarked on national economic program already in 1909. Keyder, *The Definition of Peripheral Economy*, p. 9.

114. Keyder, *State & Class in Turkey*, p. 34.

115. Çağlar Keyder, "Creation and Destruction of Forms of Manufacturing: The Ottoman Empire," in *Between Development and Underdevelopment, 1800-1870*, ed. Jean Batou, Publications du Centre d'histoire économique internationale de l'université de Genève, 6 (Geneva: Droz, 1991), p. 179; Keyder, *State & Class in Turkey*, p. 45. This notion contradicts to some extent Keyder's view that the "Anatolian bourgeoisie did not control agricultural production and was not in any position to guarantee a sustained supply of raw materials for the requirements of industrial processing." Keyder, "The Agrarian Background and the Origins of the Turkish Bourgeoisie," p. 51.

ties" who were "officially deported, leading to the well-known tragedy."[116]

While developing his argument over the years, Keyder has modified various aspects of it without changing the core. Thus, he no longer explicitly refers to the theory of the Asiatic Mode of Production, while he maintains the concept of the bureaucracy as a class. Keyder has abandoned his earlier views of the non-Muslims bourgeoisie as a comprador class, now following Kasaba's argument.[117] Keyder's acceptance of Sussnitzki's work as a major source on late Ottoman social history paved the way for his hypothesis of class formation and class struggle along ethnic lines.[118]

116. The author labels the Armenian Genocide also as "purges" and writes that the Armenians were "driven out of Anatolia" and had "perished, departed or been expelled." Çağlar Keyder, "Small Peasant Ownership in Turkey," *Review* 7, no. 1 (1983), p. 70; Keyder, "The Cycle of Sharecropping," p. 139; compare Keyder, Özveren, and Quataert, "Port Cities in the Ottoman Empire," p. 524; Keyder, "Class and State in the Transformation of Modern Turkey," pp. 198-99; Keyder, "Creation and Destruction of Forms of Manufacturing," p. 179; Çağlar Keyder, "The Genesis of Petty Commodity Production in Agriculture: The Case of Turkey," in *Culture and Economy: Changes in Turkish Villages,* ed. Paul E. Stirling (Huntingdon: Eothen Press, 1993), p. 181; Keyder, "The Agrarian Background and the Origins of the Turkish Bourgeoisie," p. 52.

117. Reşat Kasaba, Çağlar Keyder, and Faruk Tabak, "Eastern Mediterranean Port Cities and Their Bourgeoisies: Merchants, Political Projects, and Nation-States," *Review* 10 (1986), pp. 123, 128.

118. See also Keyder, Özveren, and Quataert, "Port Cities in the Ottoman Empire," p. 545. In Gökalp's scenario the class struggle took place between the Ottoman bureaucracy and the Turkish masses; see Heyd, *Foundations of Turkish Nationalism,* p. 141.

5
CONCLUSION:
NATIONALISM IN PROGRESSIVE GARB

Sussnitzki's work is still referred to by scholars who regard the thesis of a racial division of labor as a valid scholarly model in Ottoman historiography. Willingness to accept this view seems to be independent of the theoretical approach employed. Thus, modernization theory, dependency theory, the world system approach, and approaches influenced by Marxist theory have all managed to accommodate Sussnitzki's thesis. This is not to say that differences between the various models do not exist. However, the use of the models discussed here constitute examples of how nationalist and ultimately racist thought can be reconfigured successfully and placed in the center of scholarly discourse. The persistence in Turkish nationalist thinking becomes apparent in the underlying assumption of the examples discussed above, where it is consistently argued that Ottoman Armenians played an unduly important role in the Ottoman economy and thus provoked a reaction of the Muslim majority.

Modern social-history writing resembles strikingly the theses of pre–World War I German propaganda, although the modern writers employ a different vocabulary.[119] German propagandists

119. For a similar thesis see Stephan H. Astourian, "The Armenian Genocide: An Interpretation," *History Teacher* 23 (1990), p. 153 n. 60.

had to combine political and socioeconomic arguments to arrive at their conclusions; the same holds true for modern authors. In order to present Armenian economic success as an obstacle to economic development, all authors have had to employ political arguments too. Only by doing so can they overcome the apparent contradiction that a dynamically developing segment of the population should be the cause for a lack of development. To arrive at such a conclusion one has to maintain an implicit ex post facto view of the events at hand. Armenian economic success was not an obstacle to Ottoman economic development but to the nationalist program of economic turkification. This was the real problem to be overcome.

In presenting Armenian economic success as provocation, the discussion of economic history conjoins the dominant discourse on Armenians in Ottoman political history. Here Armenians are described as provocateurs who intentionally brought about their own physical demise. The subversive nature of the politics of Armenian revolutionary parties is matched by the economic subversion of the Armenian bourgeoisie. Thus, Armenian provocation of Muslims is presented as having been a more widespread phenomenon than the activities of Armenian revolutionaries alone would suggest.[120]

In sum, social history has been unable to criticize and revise Turkish nationalist views. On the contrary, it complements and reinforces these views. It might be understood as a second pillar of contemporary ethnic stereotyping on Ottoman Armenians and instrumental in the perpetuation of the dominant views on Ottoman Armenians in recent western scholarship. This underlying acquiescence of nominally non-nationalist intellectuals with Turkish nationalist historiography impedes an adequate concep-

---

120. On the "provocation thesis," see Robert F. Melson, *Revolution and Genocide: On the Origins of the Armenian Genocide and the Holocaust* (Chicago: Univ. of Chicago Press, 1992), pp. 43–69, 141–70.

tualization of the Armenian Genocide and the end of the Ottoman Empire within social history. A proper integration of crucial
events—the Armenian Genocide, the Kurdish deportations of
World War I, the destruction of the Ottoman Greek communities, and the losses of the Turkish civil population during the
forced turkification campaigns—into a critical social history of
the Ottoman social formation is still a desideratum. The development of a critical approach remains an important task, since the
definition of ethnic cleansing and genocide as a class struggle
provides a paradigm for present-day nationalists and genocidal
regimes.